Economic Stabilization and Debt in Developing Countries

The Ohlin Lectures

Economic Stabilization and Debt in Developing Countries

Richard N. Cooper

The MIT Press
Cambridge, Massachusetts
London, England

This book was set in Palatino by The MIT Press and printed and bound in the United States of America.

Library of Congress Cataloging-in-Publication Data

Cooper, Richard N.
    [Economic stabilization in developing countries]
    Economic stabilization and debt in developing countries/
Richard N. Cooper.
        p.   cm.—(Ohlin Lectures)
    Originally published: Economic stabilization in developing
countries. San Francisco, Calif.: ICS Press, c1991.
    Includes bibliographical references and index.
    ISBN 0-262-03187-6
    1. Economic stabilization—Developing countries.   2. Debts,
External—Developing countries.   3. Developing countries—
Economic policy.   I. Title.   II. Series.
HC59.C638   1991b
338.9'009172'4—dc20   91-34810
                                                                 CIP

Contents

Tables and Figures

Figures

Preface

It is a great privilege to have been asked to deliver these lectures in honor of Bertil Ohlin. Ohlin had a distinguished career in two fields, academics and politics, making important contributions to both. He was elected to the Swedish Parliament in 1938 and subsequently led the Liberal Party for over two decades in the opposition. It is a pity that he retired shortly before the Liberal Party came to power, however briefly. But Ohlin embodied an intellectual power and integrity that set a standard for other politicians and made it more difficult for them to engage in shoddy argument. At the same time, his debate with Keynes over the transfer problem (German reparations being the immediate issue under discussion) has become part of the classic lore of international economics, and his name lives on in every international economics textbook as co-author of the Heckscher-Ohlin theory of comparative advantage, based on each nation's endowments of factors of production.

This short book represents a considerably expanded version of two lectures given in Stockholm in September 1988. According to the guidelines I was given, one lecture was to be addressed to a lay audience, the other to a more specialized audience of actual and prospective economists. The material that follows still reflects this division somewhat, which explains the lack of full integration between the first three chapters of the book, which concern how developing countries dealt with the various internal and especially external shocks experienced during the period 1973–88, and the last two chapters, which cover the international debt crisis since 1982 from a global perspective.

Most macroeconomic theory was produced by economists in developed countries. But developing countries are subject to the same national balance-sheet constraints (e.g., between national income and expenditure, or in transactions with the rest of the world), and they are also subject to shocks large enough to affect the entire economy. It is therefore worthwhile to explore how those countries in fact cope with the various shocks they have experienced, and to what extent their handling of major shocks improved or worsened their subsequent economic performance. This general topic has been the subject of a major comparative study, conducted under World Bank sponsorship, of eighteen developing countries, covering the period from the mid-1960s to the late 1980s. In the first part of the book I have drawn on preliminary material from that study, which is still incomplete, and on discussions with the other principal investigators, Max Corden, Ian Little, and Sarath Rajapatirana, who have given me helpful comments on the manuscript for this book, as has Peter Kenen of Princeton University.

Chapters 4 and 5 draw heavily on the Wallenberg lecture given at Georgetown University in 1986 and published by the Georgetown Law Center as *The Lingering Problem of LDC Debt*, although the material has been extensively revised and extended in view of the important developments that have occurred in recent years in the area of international debt management.

I am grateful to the Center for International Affairs at Harvard University and to the Institute for International Economics for providing a congenial atmosphere in which to work in Cambridge and in Washington. William Cline and John Williamson of the Institute provided helpful comments on a draft of the book. I am also grateful to Jenny Gordon and to Joe Crowley for valuable research assistance in preparing these lectures for publication, and to Jenny Gordon for preparing the index.

Introduction

Macroeconomic analysis was developed in and for highly developed economies. Lively debate has taken place over the years over how active monetary and fiscal policies should be in those economies and what could reasonably be expected of those instruments in terms of stabilizing economic activity or controlling inflation. In contrast, *development economics* was developed for and in the context of poorer countries, whose principal economic concern was with raising standards of living. That subfield was oriented toward long-term growth, with much emphasis on savings, investment, and the contribution of investment to growth, as well as on the quality of the labor force. Large debates in this subfield concerned the appropriate role of government in fostering growth—in particular whether it should perform the roles of entrepreneur and manager of commercial activities—summed up somewhat misleadingly in the debate over whether socialism or capitalism offered the most effective path to economic development.

The experience of the 1970s and 1980s suggests that this dichotomy is no longer tenable, if it ever was. With the sharp worldwide slowdown in growth, developed countries became concerned with long-term growth while developing countries became preoccupied with "stabilization" and short-run macroeconomic management.[1] Still, most low-income countries desire to improve their citizens' standard of living over time, that is, they remain concerned with long-run growth. That raises the question of the connection, if any, between stabilization and growth. Does stabilization policy as practiced merely lop off the peaks and troughs around unchanged long-run trends, or do the objectives and techniques of stabilization policy influence the trend itself? This question motivated a major study commissioned by the World Bank of the experience of eighteen developing countries during the 1970s and 1980s to ascertain the links between stabilization and growth. The first three chapters offer some preliminary observations on that question, focusing their attention on the sources of the need for stabilization, the diverse national responses to those needs, and the similarly diverse economic outcomes.[2] Chapter 1 proceeds roughly chronologically, starting with the first sharp increase in oil prices in 1974, but with occasional digressions for analysis or to pull together certain topics that if presented chronologically would have disturbed the flow of the presentation. In particular, the chapter focuses first on countries that experienced adverse shocks and then returns to look at the countries that experienced apparently favorable shocks—events that typically turned out to be less favorable than they seemed at first. This chapter contains more detail than many would like, but inadequate detail for those interested in specific events in specific countries. The latter part is designed to give a flavor of the approach to macroeconomic policymaking in the countries covered, but only a flavor, and some readers may prefer to skip over it.

Chapter 2 takes up the analytics of the disabsorption that a country must undertake if foreign lending dries up or if the terms of trade move against it. This chapter also discusses how a drying up of foreign credit may evolve into inflationary pressures and looks at the role of the International Monetary Fund in designing stabilization programs for its member countries.

Chapter 3 examines whether differences in political organization, or other leading hypotheses, offer a satisfactory explanation for the substantial differences in outcome. Finally, it draws on the experience of these countries as lessons for successful stabilization and assesses the extent to which success in stabilization is conducive to long-term growth.

Chapter 4 shifts perspective from individual developing countries to the world economic system and examines the question of external debt from that perspective. It addresses the origins of the debt problem and examines why the question of external debt has proved to be such a difficult problem to resolve internationally. Chapter 5 then suggests how the debt problem is likely to be resolved. Reflecting their origins, these chapters are somewhat less technical than the two preceding them.

Economic Stabilization
and Debt in Developing
Countries

1

How Countries Coped
with External Distur-
bances

The First Oil Shock

In December 1973 the ministers of the Organization of Petroleum Exporting Countries (OPEC), hosted by the Shah of Iran
in Teheran, increased the marker price of OPEC crude oil from
$3.60 to $11.65 a barrel, a threefold increase that was to take
effect January 1, 1974. (In 1970 it had been $1.35 a barrel.) In the
course of three months, the typical payment period for contract oil, about 12 percent of world trade was redirected. On
exports of about 30 million barrels a day, payments to OPEC
members increased the equivalent of $88 billion a year.

This dramatic event—OPEC I, as we may call it—inaugurated
a period of great turbulence in the world economy, which
hardly settled down even by the end of the 1980s. Of course,
the OPEC price increase itself arose out of a period of some
turbulence: world economic growth had been unusually rapid
in 1972–73; the demand for OPEC oil had risen rapidly, from
less than 19 million barrels a day in 1968 to 30 million barrels
a day in 1973; low grain stocks, combined with a change in the

Soviet Union's agricultural strategy, set off a sharp rise in grain prices, which together with high demand sparked a general boom in primary product prices (excluding beverages); in March 1973 major currencies were let loose to float against one another, and this precipitated a partial breakdown of the postwar international monetary system; and in October 1973 the Arab oil-exporting countries embargoed the United States and the Netherlands following the brief Yom Kippur War.

OPEC I was probably the largest shock per unit time the world economy has ever experienced. It represented a major redistribution between oil-importing and oil-exporting nations and, within nations, between oil consumers and oil producers— except where, as in the United States, domestic oil prices were controlled to inhibit such redistribution. We are still living with the legacy of OPEC I—partly in the form of higher oil prices, partly through accumulated debt, and partly through the memories of the subsequent turbulence—which will influence policymaking for many years to come.[1]

OPEC I was followed by a world recession in 1974–75, the deepest and most widespread since the Great Depression of the 1930s. Rough normalcy returned by 1978, only to be broken by another shock to the oil market, which we will somewhat unfairly call OPEC II. This time, world oil prices increased by nearly a factor of three over a two-year period (see figure 1.1).[2] The world recession that followed in 1981–82 was in some respects even deeper than the one of 1974–75. Moreover, interest rates rose to unprecedented levels in the early 1980s and remained high throughout the recession, thus contribut-

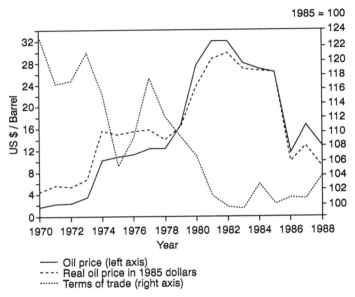

Figure 1.1
Oil prices and terms of trade of non-oil developing countries, 1970–1988

ing to, if not precipitating, a debt crisis in 1982–83. One country after another found itself unable to renew outstanding credits. For a time, many countries even stopped paying interest on their outstanding debts. During this period the U.S. dollar became exceptionally strong against other leading currencies, notably the yen and the deutsche mark, and the U.S. trade deficit zoomed; but after early 1985 the dollar took a sharp fall and the U.S. trade position began to improve, although a large deficit remained in the late 1980s. In 1986 oil prices, after slipping for several years, dropped to about one-third of their

1981 peak (in dollar terms), but by 1989 they were back up to about $18 a barrel.

In retrospect, the 1960s represented an excellent decade for the world economy, to judge by growth in output, employment, and trade at relatively low inflation (see table 1.1). In the 1970s growth began to slow down and inflation to rise, although the slowdown was more noticeable in the developed than in the developing countries. By the late 1980s inflation was brought under control and growth was revived somewhat in the developed countries, but for the developing countries the decade brought a further slowdown and higher inflation.

Table 1.1
Average rates of growth and inflation (percent per annum)

	Year	Industrial countries	Oil-producing developing countries	Non-oil developing countries
Growth[a]	1960–1973	4.7	7.4	5.1
	1973–1980	2.9	5.1	5.4
	1980–1989	2.7	0.9	4.0
Inflation[b]	1960–1973	3.7	4.3	11.4
	1973–1980	9.7	14.2	23.5
	1980–1989	5.7	10.2	48.3

a. Growth in real GDP, 1985 prices, *International Financial Statistics*. GDP at constant prices for oil, exporting developing countries from 1981 is from *World Economic Outlook 1989*; GDP prior to this is from *International Financial Statistics*, which is for all oil-exporting countries.
b. Inflation is measured by the consumer price index, *International Financial Statistics*.
Sources: IMF, *World Economic Outlook* and *International Financial Statistics*.

Impact of an Oil Price Increase

Consider an oil-importing country that is initially in equilibrium, in the sense that capital inflows (including foreign aid)
are sufficient to cover its current account deficit, inflation is
positive but not accelerating, and the budget deficit is financed
in part by foreign capital and in part by borrowing from the
central bank—in short, a typical developing country. The
extent to which a country deviates from this pattern will
influence how it responds to a sharp increase in oil prices or to
other exogenous shocks.

In the typical case, the oil price increase will first raise the
country's current account deficit and the level of wholesale
prices in the country. The demand for non-oil goods and
services will then contract, insofar as firms and households
must pay the increased price and their demand for oil is
inelastic, as it is likely to be. In these circumstances, total
expenditures on oil will rise even though the amount of oil
demanded falls, and less income will be available to purchase
other goods and services. Thus, demand will contract. In
addition, if the oil price increase is substantial, energy-using
firms that were previously profitable may now find themselves unprofitable, their capital stock prematurely obsolete,
while previously unprofitable (energy-saving) investments
will have become much more attractive.

How should the government respond, or encourage its residents to respond, to these circumstances? The conventional
view is that if the oil price increase is temporary, the country

should borrow to cover its enlarged current account deficit, cutting back domestic demand only enough to ensure servicing of the additional debt. If the price increase is thought to be durable, the country should adjust to the new circumstances, taking such steps as are necessary to reduce the now-enlarged current account deficit to the level of sustainable capital inflow, as before—moving resources out of now-unprofitable activities into newly profitable activities and adjusting the overall level of demand to the new (and reduced) level of output, after allowing for any continuing capital inflow.

Developing countries as a group have been chastised for treating a durable price increase as temporary. But this is Monday-morning quarterbacking. In many cases—and the oil price increase of 1974 was one—it is impossible to tell whether the disturbance is going to be temporary or permanent. Eminent economists at the time, including Milton Friedman in a widely read popular article, argued that OPEC was a cartel, that all cartels have proved to be temporary, and therefore the oil price increase would not endure.[3] Others argued that, although unacceptable, the situation would not go away because the OPEC countries had a stranglehold on a critical raw material for all industrial countries and, through investments, on their capital markets as well (see, for example, Levy 1974). Both these views turned out to be incorrect. But governments might be excused for not foreseeing accurately what the future would bring.

Even if an oil price increase such as this is considered durable, how rapidly should the economy be encouraged to adjust to the new situation? The case for gradualism is that it will involve a lower total cost of transferring resources from one activity to another, because resource shifts are more difficult and hence generally more costly if they have to be accomplished quickly. The total loss of output is likely to be greater. The savings in real output from a gradual adjustment to a shock must then be weighed against the costs of the borrowing required to cover the intervening excess of expenditure over output and of imports over exports. It should be noted that in a gradual approach some of the borrowing may quite appropriately serve to finance consumption, not just investment—in this case the consumption of oil. To cut non-oil consumption rapidly might incur costly and possibly unnecessary losses of output while the adjustment is taking place.

The risk of gradualism, particularly if many parties are involved, is that economic agents will not recognize the extent to which adjustment is needed, and their well-intentioned gradualism will become procrastination. Procrastination in turn is costly because debt must be accumulated to cover the excess expenditure. A political judgment is required to strike the right balance between these conflicting considerations. Formal economic analysis has little to contribute here, and economists have given the issue too little recognition.

Policymakers must decide not only on the speed of economic adjustment but also on the way it should proceed. Should they respond to the contraction in non-oil demand by introducing expansionary policies, or should they respond to the increase in prices by adopting contractionary or anti-inflationary policies? The notion that the price level could be held steady in the face of a sharp increase in oil prices through sufficiently steadfast monetary policy is an economist's fiction, much like the fiction of a physicist postulating a frictionless surface. A sufficiently tight monetary policy can probably restore the price level to what it was before the oil price increase, but only by generating a recession that is strong enough to drive other prices down enough to compensate for the increased oil price. That could be a costly action. The cost-minimizing policy in the face of a once-and-for-all increase in the price level, such as a sharp oil price increases, is probably a once-and-for-all increase in the supply of money (see Phelps 1978).

The challenge lies in persuading the relevant economic agents of the difference between a once-and-for-all increase in the price level and a rise in the rate of inflation, that is, the rate at which prices are likely to continue to increase. In the short run, these different phenomena are indistinguishable, and the risk of ratifying a once-and-for-all increase in the price level with an intended once-and-for-all increase in the money supply is that economic agents will interpret this action as inflationary and will take steps to hedge against future inflation (for example, by acquiring stocks of goods or anticipating future inflation in wage demands), thereby contributing to inflation. The authorities therefore face a serious dilemma in the presence of a substantial oil price increase, one that must be resolved through a political judgment, based in part on the ability of the authorities to make the public aware of a very subtle distinction.

Country Responses

How did developing countries actually cope with OPEC I and, indeed, with the general post-1973 turbulence? Much has been written about the countries of the Southern Cone of South America, with their distinctive economic experiments of the late 1970s, and more generally about Latin America, especially Brazil and Mexico, in the 1980s (see, for example, Edwards and Larrain 1989; Williamson 1990). But those countries' experiences turn out not to be typical of the rest of the world. A more representative view of the responses of developing countries to the shocks of these decades and of their implications for long-term growth can be found by drawing on the experiences of countries in Asia and Africa as well, eighteen in all. The sample is representative without being strictly random. It includes all developing countries with a GNP in 1987 in excess of $35 billion, apart from Egypt: Argentina, Brazil, Colombia, India, Indonesia, Korea, Mexico, Nigeria, Pakistan, Thailand, and Turkey. In addition, it includes a sampling of smaller countries: Cameroon, Chile, Costa Rica, Ivory Coast, Kenya, Morocco, and Sri Lanka. Together, these countries accounted for 60 percent of the GNP arising in all developing countries, apart from China. Such an empirical examination can discover if any useful generalizations might be made to temper the extensive a priori theorizing to which economists have become prone. Although the economists' general tool kit was used in the analysis, no attempt was made to superimpose a common model on all of these countries, on the assumption that the distinctive history and institutional setup in each was at least potentially important in determining the response of policymakers to shocks and of economic agents both to shocks and to policymakers' reactions to the shocks.

Although the countries enjoy the same basic institutions and are often exposed to common external shocks, institutions operate quite differently in each country, in part because of differences in economic and political structure and in part because of distinctive histories and ideologies that influence both public and official expectations about how the economy will respond both to exogenous shocks and to policy actions. At some risk of losing the forest for the trees, it is illuminating to describe in at least brief detail the circumstances and responses of our eighteen countries during the two major oil shocks of the 1970s, and of five countries that enjoyed a boom in coffee and cocoa prices in the late 1970s.

On the surface, the reactions to OPEC I and its associated recession appeared to be less diverse than the reactions to subsequent developments. Most countries borrowed to cover their enlarged oil deficit, although in varying degrees. Here, however, the complications of reality intrude on the clean analysis that can be done of an idealized case. Two of the countries—Indonesia and Nigeria—were substantial net exporters of oil in 1973 (Cameroon and Mexico later became net oil exporters). They therefore experienced an oil boom as a result of OPEC I.

Several countries (Argentina, Colombia, and Mexico) were more or less self-sufficient in oil, so the oil price increase did not adversely affect their current account. They were nonetheless confronted with the critical decision of whether to transmit the higher world price to the internal market, as the opportunity cost of their oil had risen with the world price. Although they could have augmented their export earnings by cutting back on domestic consumption, such an action would have entailed the difficult policy choices mentioned above. To avoid or postpone these choices, all three countries chose to retain domestic oil prices at their pre-1974 level, allowing them to rise only gradually over time. This policy, of course, required effective export controls on oil, which were easy enough to impose because the oil industry was in the hands of government enterprises in all three countries.

Several other countries found the world demand for their export products sufficiently strong to offset the increased oil bills. Thus the international terms of trade actually improved for Morocco, despite the rise in oil price, because of a strong demand for its phosphates. Chile did not experience a sharp deterioration in terms of trade until 1975, because copper prices rose in 1973–74 almost as dramatically as oil prices. These countries—along with Cameroon, Ivory Coast, India, and Thailand—faced a somewhat different and less urgent set of choices than the other eleven countries because their current account did not deteriorate (see table 1.2).[4]

In the remaining countries the oil price increase had an immediate effect on the terms of trade and on current account positions. But they also found themselves in different initial situations. Some of them were in relatively good economic shape in 1973, a year of general buoyancy in the world economy; others were in poor shape and already experiencing balance-

Table 1.2
Effect of the first oil shock, changes from 1973 to 1974

	Value of petroleum imports (% 1973 GDP)	Terms of trade %	Ratio to 1973 GDP (%)	Current account (US$ million)	Current account (% 1973 GDP)	Reserves (US$ million)
Argentina	0.9	-19.4	-1.1	-593	-1.5	-4
Brazil	2.9	-31.7	-2.8	-5,404	-6.8	-1,144
Cameroon	1.2	-18.4	-3.5	-1	-0.1	27
Chile	1.7	-27.6	-4.2	-13	-0.9	-81
Colombia	-0.5	8.5	0.9	-297	-3.1	-85
Costa Rica	2.2	-21.1	-6.3	-154	-11.2	-6
Cote d'Ivoire	3.1	-2.6	-0.7	158	6.3	-23
India	1.3	-24.7	-1.0	1,753	2.2	179
Indonesia	-19.8	108.9	18.8	1,073	6.3	685
Kenya	3.9	1.7	0.5	-182	-7.2	-40
Korea, Rep. of	4.9	-15.1	-4.7	-1,720	-12.7	-608
Mexico	0.1	-21.4	-1.5	-1,460	-2.4	77
Morocco	2.9	20.5	3.6	130	2.1	150
Nigeria	-27.3	191.7	17.4	4,905	23.9	5,044
Pakistan	2.3	-22.7	-3.5	-848	-13.4	-20
Sri Lanka	2.8	-24.1	-4.7	-111	-5.1	-9
Thailand	3.6	-5.0	-1.0	-40	-0.4	551
Turkey	2.4	-20.7	-2.0	-1,221	-5.8	-424

Note: Negative sign in first column indicates increase in net exports.
Source: World Bank data base; IMF, *International Financial Statistics*.

of-payments difficulties or inflation above acceptable levels. India fell into this category. It had suffered a severe drought in 1972/73, which had cut agricultural production and raised prices significantly. Sri Lanka was also in straitened circumstances, and Kenya was in the process of retrenching after a strong investment boom in the early 1970s that had unleashed inflation.

World economic activity slowed down in the latter half of 1974, partly because of the impact of the oil price increase itself and partly because of contractionary economic policies in the United States, the Federal Republic of Germany, and Japan (following a startling spring wage offensive by Japanese workers). That broke the price boom for most commodities and put the brakes on world trade in goods, such as rubber and copper, that are sensitive to changes in industrial production. At the same time, a severe frost in Brazil in July 1975 sent world coffee prices sharply up for two years, thus greatly improving the export earnings of the coffee producers in our sample— Cameroon, Colombia, Costa Rica, Ivory Coast, and Kenya.

The range of responses was wide, although all eighteen countries ended up borrowing abroad to a considerable extent. Costa Rica, Pakistan, and Turkey—as well as Brazil after a brief monetary and fiscal retrenchment in early 1974—all but ignored the oil price increase in their macroeconomic policy and simply borrowed abroad to cover the bill. Pakistan borrowed mainly from the newly oil-rich, fellow-Moslem countries, and on favorable terms. The others borrowed mainly on commercial terms from the large banks of the world. Brazil launched a major investment program to divert demand away from oil in the long run—toward hydroelectric and nuclear power and toward ethanol (made largely from sugar, which Brazil produces in abundance) for automotive use. Some of this investment turned out to be unprofitable, but it seemed prudent at the time, and that prudence seemed to be rewarded at the time of the second oil shock.

Thailand took some contractionary monetary and fiscal action in early 1974, but that seems to have been directed more at the inflation of 1973 than at the emergence of a larger payments deficit. As the world economy went into its slump, Thailand fostered public investments, as did Costa Rica, Ivory Coast, and Turkey. In other words, these countries pursued a policy that attempted to stabilize the growth in real demand.

Sri Lanka tightened import restrictions, cut food subsidies, and introduced rationing. Unlike most other countries, it did not attempt to borrow from commercial banks, expecting no doubt to be turned down because its reserves were low and its socialist government emphasized helping the poor. Its foreign exchange reserves were too small to cover more than a fraction of the increased oil import bill, so it cut total imports sharply. But it did borrow extensively from international organizations, including the Compensatory Financing Facility of the International Monetary Fund (IMF), to cover shortfalls in export earnings, and the newly created IMF Oil Facility. Moreover, Sri Lanka was one of only four countries in our list that went to the IMF in 1974 for an ordinary loan, under the usual macroeconomic conditionality. Its import compression and a sharp rise in the world prices of tea and copra produced a current account surplus by 1977.

Kenya, like Sri Lanka and Brazil, increased import restrictions. It also continued the tight credit policy that it had introduced as part of its anti-inflation program in 1973, cut back on public investment (but that was offset by a growth in public consumption), and devalued the Kenyan shilling by 14 percent in 1975 as part of an IMF program undertaken in that year of world recession.

Korea postponed the implementation of a large investment program it had launched in 1973 and tightened domestic credit. But its principal emphasis was on stimulating exports, including contract construction in the newly rich Middle Eastern countries, and to that end it introduced various export incentives (mainly cheap credit) and devalued the Korean won by 22 percent in December 1974. It was so successful in this effort that the current account deficit of $2 billion in 1974 and 1975 dropped to $300 million by 1976 and disappeared altogether in 1977.

As already mentioned, India was preoccupied with inflation, which had exceeded the politically critical level of 10 percent in 1973 and then jumped to more than 25 percent in 1974, in part because of the oil price increase but more because of the drought. India pursued stringent fiscal and monetary contraction, raising both taxes and bank liquidity requirements, which along with a better harvest brought inflation below zero in 1975.

In response to the inflationary excesses of the previous Allende administration, the new Chilean military government introduced draconian monetary and fiscal measures, reinforced after the collapse of copper prices in late 1974. It also depreciated sharply the Chilean peso, all in the context of an IMF program initiated early in 1974.

Many oil-importing countries attempted to resolve their policy dilemmas by controlling domestic oil prices, or at least moderating the increase. Such action was made easier by the fact that distribution of oil products was a state monopoly in many developing countries and in others was in the hands of relatively few large private suppliers. But this action solves a short-run problem only by creating two long-run ones: there is no price incentive for the public to conserve oil, and the government must somehow make up the difference between the high price of imported oil and the controlled domestic price. The U.S. government accomplished this by controlling the price of domestically produced oil and blending it through a complicated allocation system with higher-priced imported oil. But this option was not available to countries that produced no domestic oil. These countries had to subsidize the price difference, which put further strain on the budget because they had to seek additional borrowing abroad or inflationary finance from the central bank.

External Borrowing

Half of the eighteen countries were heavy borrowers abroad, in that the ratio of external debt to GDP rose by 5 percentage points or more between 1973 and 1978 (see table 1.3). But in several cases—Cameroon, Ivory Coast, Mexico, and Morocco, in each of which the ratio of external public borrowing to GDP grew by more than 12 percentage points between 1973 and 1978—the growth in external debt cannot be attributed to the oil shock. Each of these countries had undertaken sizable public investment projects in the mid-1970s (largely for political reasons in the cases of Ivory Coast and Morocco and to help develop their oil resources in the cases of Cameroon and Mexico). In Argentina, Brazil, Costa Rica, Kenya, and Sri

Table 1.3
Publicly guaranteed external debt as a percentage of GDP

Country	1973	1978	1983	1988
Argentina	7.1	15.7	39.2	53.7
Brazil	9.8	15.2	28.6	25.3
Cameroon	13.5	26.4	23.5	22.8
Chile	27.2	28.3	33.4	62.3
Colombia	19.0	12.1	17.7	35.6
Costa Rica	16.3	26.9	99.4	74.7
Cote d'Ivoire	23.1	35.4	72.0	83.0
India	13.0	12.2	11.7	18.4
Indonesia	30.6	24.3	25.3	49.3
Kenya	20.6	26.2	40.6	49.3
Korea, Republic of	26.2	22.6	26.9	12.5
Mexico	9.3	23.3	44.8	47.0
Morocco	16.1	39.9	77.5	84.4
Nigeria	5.5	3.7	13.4	96.3
Pakistan	66.9	41.9	33.1	36.5
Sri Lanka	22.2	35.4	40.1	59.0
Thailand	4.1	7.3	17.4	23.1
Turkey	13.7	12.3	31.4	43.8

Source: World Bank data base (GDP calculated in of U.S. dollars) and *World Debt Tables*.

Lanka, the borrowing was intended partly to cover oil bills and partly to finance investment. Most of Sri Lanka's heavy borrowing came after the defeat of the socialist government in 1977 and, as noted, Brazil, Costa Rica, and Korea all had major investment programs going in the mid-1970s, of which only Brazil's borrowing can be directly related to the oil shock.

The extensive borrowing was made possible by two developments, one evolutionary and the other directly related to the oil shock. The first was the creation in 1957 of the Eurodollar market—a market in short-term dollar funds based in London and by 1974 including most of the world's leading banks. This market grew steadily throughout the 1960s, and by the early 1970s an increasing number of developing countries had acquired access to it. At the same time, banks had begun to lend at longer maturities. Thus, three-year loans had become quite common, and even five-year loans existed.

After the sharp rise in oil prices, the oil-exporting countries found themselves earning money faster than they could spend it. They placed some of it in U.S. Treasury securities, which enjoyed high safety and high liquidity, but they also deposited some with banks in the Eurodollar market and thereby provided the wherewithal for a great increase in bank lending. The OPEC members launched major spending programs, but they could not spend all of their increased income at once, in part because their infrastructure could not initially handle a large increase in the volume of imports (ships sometimes waited for months to unload their goods in Nigeria and Saudi Arabia, for instance). OPEC members together ran a current account surplus of $60 billion in 1974, which declined gradually to $5 billion in 1978, as their spending gradually rose to match their enlarged income.

As funds became more available, real interest rates declined, reflecting the temporary increase in world saving rates as real income was transferred from oil consumers to oil-producing countries that were temporarily high savers because of their inability to spend rapidly. Developing countries that were still relatively new to the Eurodollar market paid a substantial premium—as high as 2 percent—over the London interbank offered rate (Libor). Borrowing to cover oil bills was not altogether irrational under the circumstances, and indeed it was the policy followed by many smaller industrialized countries. Sweden explicitly pursued an overbridge policy that did not allow the oil price increase to deflect Sweden from its normal path of growth. These countries also borrowed heavily in the Eurodollar market. The classical mechanism was at work: higher world savings led to lower world interest rates, which led to increased borrowing both for consumption and for investment. Such borrowing was instrumental in mitigating the depth of the 1975 recession, which would have been much more severe without the stimulus to demand supported by borrowing. This was also the period, however, in which many countries began to incur serious debts, and although some concern was expressed at the time, on the whole the debts were considered quite manageable (see, for example, Gardner et al. 1975).

A complicating factor in interpreting the response to OPEC I was the general atmosphere in many developing countries at the time. Buoyed by the relative success of the 1960s, many developing countries felt confidant that they had mastered the art of development planning and could become more ambitious. They also had increasing access to the growing international money and capital market centered in London, at moderate commercial interest rates. Thus, more than two-thirds of the eighteen countries launched substantial investment programs in the mid-1970s, in nine cases increasing the ratio of investment to GDP by more than 5 percentage points. As a result, the increased foreign borrowing was almost always associated with increased investment, often planned or even started *before* the increase in oil prices.

Curiously, many developing countries also officially welcomed the increase in oil prices, even when it worsened their own financial position. They saw it as an instrument that was at last bringing some developing countries (OPEC members) to the attention of the rich industrialized nations. They saw prices as a powerful bargaining lever in international negotiations over the nature and structure of the international economic order, which would tilt that order more in favor of the developing world. This expectation proved to be in vain, not so much because OPEC lost control of oil prices during the second oil shock, but because OPEC interests differed considerably from those of the relatively poorer oil-importing countries. Also, as the examples of Korea and other countries demonstrate, the world economic system was already highly permissive with respect to economic development for any country willing to take advantage of what that system had to offer and to adapt its own policies accordingly. In short, many of the proposals for improvement put forward by the developing countries during the 1970s turned out, on close inspection, to be inferior to existing arrangements (Cooper 1977; Little 1982).

By 1978 world growth had been restored, OPEC members had learned how to spend their higher incomes, and oil-importing developing countries generally had maintained their growth through the oil shock, albeit at the expense of building up substantial but still manageable levels of external debt.

The Second Oil Shock

The dynamics of OPEC II were quite different from those of OPEC I, but the macroeconomic effects were similar. The world oil market was relatively calm by mid-1978, and oil prices had actually declined somewhat in real terms from 1974. Oil users felt sufficiently comfortable to draw down their oil stocks during the course of 1978. Then turmoil developed in Iran. Oil-field workers went on strike in December 1978, and about 5 million barrels a day of oil production was temporarily lost. Political confusion reigned for several weeks. In January the Shah left Iran in the hands of government officials, and shortly thereafter the Ayatollah Khomeini arrived and proclaimed an Islamic Republic. Iranian oil production increased, but rarely reached half of its previous levels. In the meantime, oil firms dependent on Iranian crude oil informed their customers that under the circumstances they could not fulfill their contracts, and prices in the oil spot market—which had grown in importance since 1973 but still accounted for less than 10 percent of the world oil trade—shot up sharply. Oil production in Saudi Arabia and other Arab oil-producing countries increased, but only after panic had set in on the world oil market. In the event, world oil production during 1979 actually exceeded final consumption by about 1 million barrels a day, the difference going into higher stocks.

Spot prices continued to rise as OPEC ministers met quarterly to quarrel over how much posted prices should be increased, and the oil market remained chaotic for many months, in the sense that many different prices prevailed for comparable oil. From late 1978 to March 1981, OPEC's posted prices rose by 150 percent, from $13 to $33 a barrel at the peak (although spot prices briefly reached $40 a barrel).

In September 1980 Iraq invaded Iran, putting both restored Iranian production and Iraqi production in jeopardy. The spot market responded briefly, but by this time oil stocks were sufficiently large and increased Saudi production pledged sufficiently early to avoid any durable effect on the oil market. The contrast with early 1979 was striking.

With such a large price increase, admittedly spread over twenty-four months, oil-importing countries once again found themselves facing the same dilemmas that OPEC I had thrown at them—with two important differences. First, external debt levels were considerably higher relative to GDP in 1980 than they had been in 1973, and a higher portion of the debt was at market interest rates, mainly but not exclusively the liabilities to commercial banks. Moreover, most of the bank debt was at floating interest rates, whereby at (usually) six-month intervals the interest rate on outstanding debt was adjusted to the changes in Libor or the U.S. prime rate that had taken place in the meantime. This feature was later to prove of considerable importance. Second, the United States tightened its monetary policy—which sets the tone for world monetary conditions—more severely in 1979–80 than it had in 1974. In particular, the basis for monetary action was shifted from interest rates to money supply in October 1979, and the consequence in an inflationary environment was much higher nominal interest rates.

As they had been forced to do after OPEC I, oil-importing countries had to decide how much to contract imports and how much to borrow to cover the increased import bill. In most cases, contracting imports implied a contraction in economic activity, because past import-substituting policies had already squeezed out most of those imports that were not related directly to production, investment, or feeding the population. Those countries that saw an opportunity also addressed the possibilities for expanding exports. As before, the oil-exporting countries had large surpluses that they placed temporarily in the Eurodollar market, and the leading industrial countries—the United States, Japan, and Germany, this time joined by Britain (which in the meantime had become a significant exporter of oil from the North Sea)—contracted monetary and fiscal policy to combat the inflationary impulses that the second oil shock had stirred throughout the world economy. But now they were joined by a number of smaller industrial countries, and even by some developing countries, so the contraction was even greater than it had been in 1974, although this did not become fully evident until 1982.

The principal difference in the outcome of OPEC II was that the combination of accumulated debt, higher interest rates, and a deep recession in 1981–82 produced a severe debt crisis for many developing countries. Some debt problems also emerged in Eastern Europe in 1981 when political difficulties in Poland raised the fears of a Russian incursion to restore order. Western banks virtually ceased lending to any country in Eastern Europe, thereby putting several countries into default as due debts could not be rolled over. Other countries, such as Turkey in 1978 and Costa Rica in 1981, had their own brand of debt problems. But the worldwide debt crisis came to a head when Mexico, ironically an oil-exporting country, declared in August 1982 that it could no longer service its commercial debt on schedule.

As a result, banks grew reluctant to lend new funds to other Latin American countries, countries in Africa, or the Philippines. Unable to borrow additional funds abroad, governments were left with fewer alternatives and more difficult choices.

The sharp recession—industrial production in the industrialized countries fell by 9 percent between early 1980 and the end of 1982—weakened the demand for most primary products, oil and non-oil alike, and oil prices fell from their 1981 peaks. The price reduction was beneficial to oil-importing countries, but of course it hurt oil-exporting countries, especially Mexico and Nigeria, which were already spending at levels beyond their greatly increased income. The prices of manufactured goods continued to rise, reflecting the delayed reaction to the oil and other price increases of 1980, so the terms of trade of many developing countries grew much worse, by 8.2 percent between 1980 and 1982 for the non-oil-exporting countries taken together.

In addition, interest rates remained exceptionally high for a recession period (table 1.4). The U.S. Treasury bill rate averaged 7.2 percent during 1978, but rose to 10 percent in 1979 and reached 14 percent in early 1980. (Eurodollar rates were typically a percentage point higher, but rose 2.5 percentage points higher in 1980–82). Interest rates dropped in mid-1980, but then rose sharply. The Treasury bill rate reached a peak of 16.3 percent in May 1981, before gradually receding to 12 percent in June 1982 and then dropping to 8 percent at the end of 1982, in the depths of the recession. Nominal interest rates were already at the double-digit level in 1979, so countries knew that they were borrowing at high rates during the period 1979–82. This was not a shock to the new borrowers, although it would have been for those with a floating-rate debt at the end of 1978. Rather, the shock (against the background of recent experience) was that short-term, real interest rates became strongly positive in 1981–82 as the oil-led price increases (predictably!) receded, and that they continued to rise (figure 1.2). Both the experience of 1974–75 and the analytical observation that large (although temporary) OPEC surpluses should drive the short-term rate of interest down led many borrowers

Table 1.4
U.S. interest rates and the change in the producer price index
(percentage)

Year	Three-month U.S. Treasury bill	Producer price—index crude materials	Producer price—index finished goods
1970	6.4	3.8	3.4
1971	4.3	2.3	2.9
1972	4.1	10.8	3.1
1973	7.0	36.6	9.3
1974	7.9	12.7	15.1
1975	5.8	0.3	11.0
1976	5.0	2.9	4.3
1977	5.3	3.3	6.5
1978	7.2	12.1	7.8
1979	10.0	17.0	11.1
1980	11.6	10.9	13.5
1981	14.1	8.1	9.3
1982	10.7	-3.0	4.0
1983	8.6	1.3	1.6
1984	9.6	2.2	2.1
1985	7.5	-7.4	0.9
1986	6.0	-8.5	-1.3
1987	5.8	6.8	2.1
1988	6.7	2.5	2.4
1989	8.1	7.4	5.2

Source: Council of Economic Advisers, *Economic Report of the President*, 1990.

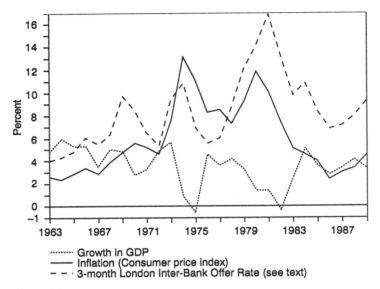

Figure 1.2
Growth, inflation, and interest rates: Industrial countries

to expect lower real interest rates. The degree of their surprise depended of course on their expectations concerning inflation in the near future.

The surprise was compounded by the fact that short-term interest rates did not fall sharply during the deep recession—contrary to all previous experience. In earlier recessions short-term interest rates had reached zero or even negative levels in real terms. This time debtors had to face the declining export prices typical of a recession without a mitigating fall in interest rates. As we shall see, few countries had anticipated the recession itself and so were particularly hard hit when the normal partial hedge for debtors against a recession—being able to borrow at low interest rates—was for the first time absent. Note that real interest rates *measured in terms of exports* were even higher for many exporters of primary products, whose prices actually declined in 1982 and rose by only 1 percent in 1983. Furthermore, borrowing rates in the London market fell by less than U.S. Treasury bill rates, owing to the enlargement of the risk premium in a world that suddenly looked very uncertain.

Country Responses

When the eighteen countries are grouped according to the nature and the magnitude of their responses, we find considerable variation in the effects of both the oil price shock and the general terms of trade shock (table 1.5). A comparison with table 1.2 suggests that the cumulative oil shock was slightly greater in 1979–81 than in 1974, but that it was spread over two years instead of a single quarter. And the terms of trade shock was of roughly the same magnitude during the two episodes.[5] Five countries benefited from the oil price increase, one of these (Argentina) only modestly. Only two countries, Indonesia and Kenya, saw an improvement in their current account between 1978 and 1981, but Kenya is surprising in view of the sharp drop in coffee prices over the period. Cameroon, Mexico, and Nigeria all increased their imports by more than the increase in oil revenues.[6]

Table 1.5
Effect of the second oil shock: Changes from 1978 to 1981

Country	Value of petroleum imports (% 1978 GDP)	Terms of trade %	Ratio to 1978 GDP %	Current account (US $mil)	Percent of 1978 GDP	Foreign exchange reserves (US$ mil)
Argentina	-0.1	-6.2	-0.5	-6568	-4.6	-1698
Brazil	3.1	-32.9	-2.5	-4715	-0.8	-5223
Cameroon	-22.6	-17.7	-4.0	-294	-1.5	33
Chile	2.3	-9.3	-2.0	-3645	-4.8	2123
Colombia	1.8	-23.5	-2.9	-2219	-2.3	2374
Costa Rica	2.2	-17.8	-6.1	-46	-1.0	-62
Cote d'Ivoire	2.5	-30.3	-8.8	-572	-2.6	-430
India	3.3	-7.4	-0.5	-3382	-0.8	-1733
Indonesia	-15.0	58.1	10.2	847	1.1	2388
Kenya	5.3	-13.9	-4.5	102	0.4	-121
Korea, Rep. of	10.3	-13.7	-4.1	-3561	-2.3	-82
Mexico	-10.8	27.2	2.0	-12890	-2.8	2233
Morocco	5.1	-10.3	-2.3	-507	-1.0	-389
Nigeria	-11.1	89.1	18.1	-2435	-0.8	2009
Pakistan	4.3	-12.6	-2.2	-196	-0.4	314
Sri Lanka	7.7	-27.2	-9.4	-378	-4.5	-70
Thailand	7.6	-23.2	-5.1	-1417	-1.8	-277
Turkey	4.5	-24.8	-2.1	-650	-0.2	127

Note: A negative sign in the first column indicates an increase in net exports from 1978.
Source: World Bank data base; IMF, *International Financial Statistics*, 77a.d., 11d.

Argentina and Chile stand out, in that each was engaged in a distinctive, risky, and ultimately unsuccessful effort to reduce inflation by fixing the foreign exchange rates of their currencies for the indefinite future—at 39 pesos to the U.S. dollar in June 1979 in Chile and on a preannounced schedule of monthly devaluation (*tablita*) starting in January 1979 in Argentina. In addition, Chile liberalized imports extensively and reduced tariffs, and Argentina introduced more modest planned liberalization. Both countries allowed the free movement of capital, although Chile placed restrictions on short-term capital inflows. Chile had pursued an austere fiscal policy for several years and ran a budget surplus of about 5 percent of GDP in 1979 and 1980, which continued into 1981 at a lower level. Argentina, in contrast, ran a deficit of about 3 percent of GDP in 1979–80, which rose to 8 percent in 1981. Each country experienced a substantial real appreciation of its currency from the end of 1978 to the end of 1980 (34 percent for Chile and 82 percent for Argentina).[7] Both countries experienced a sharp deterioration in the current account between 1978 and 1981, by $3.7 billion (9 percent of GDP) in Chile and by $6.6 billion (3 percent of GDP) in Argentina, to which oil price increases contributed only a small part. Argentina's situation was complicated by a void in economic policy in the six months before General Roberto Viola assumed the presidency in March 1981. During this time large amounts of Argentine capital left the country, despite high real interest rates on domestic assets, on the expectation that the *tablita* policy would not survive.[8] This expectation proved to be correct, even after allowing for a devaluation in early 1981 that was not preannounced. Chile had failed to de-index its wage contracts, which were based on the previous price movements, so that real wages rose sharply as inflation slowed down (Corbo et al. 1986). Both countries introduced extensive policy changes in 1982, related in part to Argentina's loss of the Falklands War with Britain and to Chile's internal financial crisis.

Brazil undertook a major currency devaluation at the end of 1979 in order to stimulate exports; but under Planning Minister Delfim Netto it adopted a policy of domestic expansion for the next year and a half, followed in 1981 by a rather orthodox stabilization policy involving monetary and fiscal contraction (see Bacha in Williamson 1983). Basically, however, Brazil borrowed its way through the second oil shock, despite the high prevailing interest rates.

So did Colombia and Morocco, with the important difference that Colombia started with a substantial current account surplus in 1978, which it transformed into a deficit equal to 4 percent of GDP by 1981, whereas Morocco started with a current account deficit equal to 10 percent of GDP, which remained essentially unchanged through the next four years. Colombia, a modest net oil exporter, introduced a macroeconomic stimulus after the decline of the coffee boom in 1978; Morocco reduced public investment in 1978 but expanded it again in 1980 with the rise in phosphate prices, despite the sharp increase in its oil bill. Its inward remittances rose sharply, and it received some aid from OPEC members, but not nearly enough to cover its increased oil payments.

India had another bad drought in 1979, but it had ample foreign exchange reserves and therefore, in contrast to 1974, maintained its expansionist stance—influenced no doubt by domestic political developments. As a result, it also borrowed through the second oil shock, largely from official sources.

Costa Rica, Ivory Coast, and Sri Lanka all cut back on (exceptionally large) public investment programs, and Costa Rica devalued its currency in 1981. All three tightened credit eventually, but none sought a major retrenchment to deal with the oil shock, and all borrowed extensively as long as they could. The debt crisis hit Costa Rica in early 1981, before Mexico and most other countries. (Its last bank consortium loan was in October 1980.)

Thailand and Pakistan had already undertaken monetary and fiscal restraint in 1978, in the latter case with IMF assistance. Pakistan was responding to a cutoff in U.S. aid (imposed because of Pakistan's nuclear program), and Thailand was attempting to restrain inflation. Thailand devalued its currency in 1981, and Pakistan introduced a managed float along with some depreciation in 1982. Pakistan received substantial aid from Arab oil-exporting countries and also increased remittances from workers in the Middle East. That assistance, along with the restraint measures and the currency depreciation, enabled Pakistan to accumulate a small current account surplus in 1983.

Kenya undertook a large cut in public investment after 1980, devalued the shilling in 1981 and again in 1982, and tightened credit substantially in 1982, but only after a lot of external borrowing had occurred.

Korea introduced a major stabilization policy in March 1979, out of concern for growing inflationary pressures from its heavy investment program and (under a fixed dollar exchange rate) the concomitant decline in its export competitiveness. The second oil shock simply reinforced the desirability of the policy in Korean eyes. With the assassination of President Park Chung Hee in November 1979, Korea entered a period of political uncertainty, which, in combination with the contractionary monetary and fiscal actions, the oil shock, and an exceptionally poor agricultural harvest, ushered in the recession of 1980, the only downturn Korea had experienced since the policy reforms of the mid-1960s. Monetary and fiscal policy became expansionary in late 1980 to combat the growing unemployment—and in time to mitigate the impact of the 1981–82 world recession—but turned contractionary again in 1983–84 to reduce inflation. The government devalued the won in January 1980 in order to reverse the real currency appreciation that had taken place since the previous devaluation in 1974 and to stimulate exports to help pay for the sharply higher oil bill. Under the pressure of the investment boom, the higher oil prices, and the poor harvest in 1980, Korea borrowed extensively in 1979–81, but its external borrowing receded sharply after that.

In 1980 Turkey, too, announced a major policy change that included substantial devaluation, monetary and fiscal contraction, and higher interest rates. But this policy package was more in response to the political and economic turmoil of the preceding three years, including accelerating inflation and civil disorder, than to the oil shock as such, even though oil accounted for nearly half of Turkey's import payments in 1980. Turkey also received considerable assistance from the international community, including the IMF, and continued to borrow extensively throughout the 1980s, although on a smaller scale than in 1975–81.

Between 1978 and 1983 the external debt-to-GDP ratio increased by more than 5 percentage points in twelve of our eighteen countries (compared with nine in the period 1973–78, following the first oil shock: see table 1.3).[9] Curiously, a number of countries that appeared to benefit from the oil price increase—Mexico and Nigeria in our group, along with Venezuela and Ecuador, but not Indonesia and Cameroon— also had to retrench in the early 1980s. The same was true for the five countries in our group that enjoyed a sharp increase in coffee prices during 1976. I therefore turn briefly to the question of how an export boom can lead to trouble.

An Export Boom: Oil

Indonesia, Mexico, and Nigeria were large net exporters of petroleum at the time of the 1979–80 oil price increase and so enjoyed a big improvement in their export earnings. Surprisingly, Mexico's current account deficit increased steadily from 1978 to 1982, right through the period of rising oil prices, even though its production and exports of oil were growing rapidly. The volume of oil exports rose fourfold from 1978 to 1982, and the value increased from $1.8 billion in 1978 to $16.7 billion in 1982. Mexico borrowed abroad, against the expectation of high future oil revenue, to finance a general investment and consumption boom, as well as the costly development of offshore oil. With the rapid escalation of both production and prices, Mexico gave apparently no thought to the question of future debt servicing and allowed the current account deficit to reach 5 percent of GDP in 1981, the year oil prices reached their peak. At the same time, Mexican citizens invested heavily abroad, speculating (correctly) that the fixed exchange rate of the peso could not be held in the face of accelerating domestic inflation.

Investment and consumption also boomed in Nigeria on the strength of increased oil revenues after 1974, but infrastructure bottlenecks delayed the arrival of imports. The current account became positive in 1979 and 1980, the years of large oil price increases, but turned negative again in 1982–83 when imports rose sharply and, more important, the production and export of petroleum dropped by a third from the levels of 1980. Oil consumers learned how to use the heavier and cheaper crude oil from Mexico, Venezuela, and elsewhere and shifted their demand from the more expensive Nigerian light oil. Yet Nigeria was reluctant to drop the high premiums that light oil had commanded in 1980. In 1981 Nigeria ran a current account deficit in excess of 6 percent of GDP, an astonishing turnaround from the 7 percent surplus of 1980.

Indonesia, like Nigeria, experienced a temporary current account surplus in 1979–80 before returning to a moderate deficit again in 1981. Unlike Mexico, Indonesia witnessed a decline in oil production and exports after the peak of 1978. But it had presciently devalued the rupiah in November 1978 to reverse the erosion of competitiveness in its non-oil exports. Exports other than oil therefore grew rapidly in 1979–80, contributing to the surpluses of those years, and remained at a high level after dipping in the 1981–82 recession. In contrast, non-oil exports of Nigeria had become negligible by the end of 1982. Indonesia maintained tighter control on government spending in the presence of vastly increased oil revenues than did

Mexico and Nigeria. Whereas Indonesian government expenditures rose by 175 percent between 1978 and 1982, Mexico's rose by a factor of seven, and Nigeria's became so chaotic that reported totals, which show an increase of only 25 percent between 1978 and 1981, are completely unreliable for this period and for several years thereafter.

In sharp contrast, Cameroon initially sequestered most of its oil revenues, investing them abroad rather than taking them into government revenues. Indeed, the oil revenues of Cameroon are a state secret, known to relatively few individuals. This invites corruption by those in the know, but it has the advantage of preventing the reckless spending that often follows a large and sudden increase in revenues. Kuwait, not in our group of countries, also sequestered oil revenues abroad, in its Fund for Future Generations, which was not to be drawn upon until the twenty-first century. The fund also retained all earnings on its foreign investments. In this way, neither the oil revenues so invested nor the earnings on them entered the Kuwaiti economy.

Obviously a boom is not an unambiguous benefit if it leads to loss of budgetary control or to debt levels that become unsustainable. Although the outcome of the oil boom was particularly dramatic, other booms have had a similar impact, such as the phosphate boom in Morocco in the mid-1970s or the coffee boom in the coffee-exporting countries in 1975 to 1978. The latter had a significant effect on five of the countries in our group: Cameroon, Colombia, Costa Rica, Ivory Coast, and Kenya.

An Export Boom: Coffee

The shake-up of the coffee market began in July 1975, when serious frost hit the coffee-producing areas of Brazil, which were not expected to recover possibly for several years. Although the frost killed many trees, which take about four years from planting to reach their first yield, the permanent damage turned out to be less than initially reported. It has been suggested (by the *Economist*) that the predictions were deliberately exaggerated to maximize Brazil's return from sales out of undamaged production and out of stocks. In any case, world coffee prices climbed from 72.5 U.S. cents per pound in 1975 to 384 cents per pound in early 1977, a fivefold increase, and 229 cents on average for the year 1977. Brazil's coffee exports in 1976 were actually 3 percent higher than they had been in 1975, partly out of stocks, but they fell 36 percent in 1977 and did not resume their volume of the mid-1970s until 1980.

The jump in coffee prices brought an unexpected bonanza to other coffee exporters. Among our five countries, coffee exports in 1975 ranged from 3 percent of GDP (Kenya) to 7.4 percent (Ivory Coast). A trebling of world coffee prices thus represented a substantial boost to each of these countries, not only to the coffee producers but to the economies as a whole.

The world prices of cocoa and tea also rose during this period, although less sharply than those of coffee. Tea prices, especially relevant to Kenya, rose 130 percent between 1975 and 1977, and cocoa prices, especially relevant to Ivory Coast, rose

120 percent (see figure 1.3). The potential impact of the three beverages together ranged from 10 percent of GDP for Kenya to a startling 31 percent for Ivory Coast (see table 1.6). But the price effect was complicated by changes in export volume, which increased substantially in Kenya but decreased in the other countries. In Colombia, for example, the volume of coffee exports fell by 40 percent, thus intensifying the world shortage.

The five countries pursued different strategies to pass the world price increases on to their coffee farmers, who are typically smallholders. In Costa Rica and Kenya, farmers received the full price increase, except for a 10 percent export

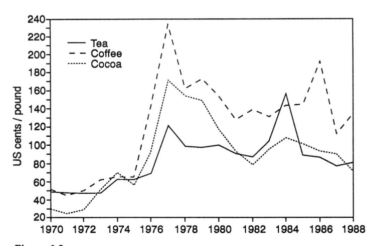

Figure 1.3
Commodity prices, 1970–1988: Beverages

Table 1.6
Performance of five coffee exporters, 1975–1978 (percentage)

	Cameroon	Colombia	Costa Rica	Cote d'Ivoire	Kenya
Coffee/ 1975 GDP	4.8	5.4	4.9	7.4	3.0
Other beverages/ 1975 GDP[a]	5.1	0.0	0.0	5.7	1.9
External disturbance/ 1975 GDP[b]	22.9	13.9	12.8	30.8	9.5
Average inflation, 1975–1978	12.7	23.5	7.8	16.0	15.6
Increase in $ imports	24.5	20.5	19.2	25.2	23.8
Change in :					
CA/GDP 1975–1977	-1.2	2.4	3.7	7.6	9.2
Average real GDP growth	5.8	4.9	5.7	8.9	7.2
Investment/ GDP	4.0	1.7	1.0	5.8	4.7
Government revenue/ GDP	2.8	-0.5	1.0	7.0	3.7
Government expenditure/ GDP	-0.4	-0.8	4.0	1.5	1.3

a. Other beverages are cocoa (New York and London) for Cote d'Ivoire and Cameroon, and tea (average auction London) for Kenya.
b. The external disturbance was calculated as the relative change in coffee price (1977–1975)/1975 (other milds New York) times share coffee exports in GDP plus the impact of other beverages. This approach assumes export volumes remained constant. Coffee prices rose by 259 percent, cocoa by 204 percent, and tea by 95 percent.
Source: IMF, *International Financial Statistics*, national accounts.

tax in Costa Rica. (In contrast, the increased revenues from the oil boom invariably accrued to governments.) In Colombia, the National Coffee Fund, a quasi-governmental organization representing coffee growers, mediates between world market developments and the growers, paying them less than the world price in periods of high prices and more in periods of low prices. In 1975–76, roughly 75 percent of the increase in world prices was passed on to growers; indeed, domestic prices rose somewhat more quickly than world prices did, reaching their peak in the fall of 1976. Like Costa Rica, Colombia imposed an export tax, and the National Coffee Fund retained the remainder of the increases.

Cameroon and Ivory Coast each have a governmental commodity stabilization fund that insulates growers from world price fluctuations and also collects taxes on sales of coffee and cocoa. While world prices were trebling between 1975 and 1977, for instance, coffee prices for Cameroon growers increased by only 38 percent for arabica and 72 percent for robusta, the two main kinds of coffee produced in the country. Domestic coffee prices increased by 10–20 percent a year throughout the 1970s, slowing to 3–10 percent a year in the 1980s, regardless of movements in the world price. During the high-price years of 1976–77, therefore, coffee producers received only about 30 percent of the export price, with the remainder accruing to the government; during years of low world coffee prices, growers received about 50 percent (Connolly 1989, p. 138 and *passim*).

Ivory Coast pursued a similar stabilization policy through CAISSTAB, an organization that buys coffee and cocoa from growers at a set price and sells the produce on the world market. During the 1970s growers received on average about 55 percent of the world price for cocoa and 51 percent of the world price for coffee. After deducting its operating costs, CAISSTAB turned the surplus over to the government. These funds financed more than half of public investment expenditure between 1975 and 1980 (Hiey 1987, pp. 8–9).

It should be noted that for analytical purposes all of these countries had essentially fixed exchange rates during the late 1970s: Cameroon and Ivory Coast were pegged to the French franc through the Communauté Financière Africaine (CFA) monetary zones of which each was a member, Kenya to the special drawing right (SDR), and Costa Rica to the U.S. dollar.[10] Colombia allowed its currency to depreciate at a steady pace against the U.S. dollar, mainly to compensate for differences in rates of inflation; the peso depreciated by 24 percent between the end of 1975 and the end of 1978. Major currencies were floating against one another during this period, so fixity against the franc or the SDR implied some movement against the dollar, but the movements were small in comparison with those of the 1980s.

Because of these exchange rate arrangements, over the three years all five countries experienced substantial increases in international reserves, supplies of money (24 to 32 percent a year), nominal and real GDP, and rates of inflation. Except for Costa Rica, whose prices were subject to price control and therefore whose index is suspect, these countries experienced double-digit inflation, despite relatively fixed exchange rates in all cases except Colombia. None of this is surprising.

Nor is it surprising that government revenues rose significantly during the coffee boom, in all cases more rapidly than nominal GDP. In relation to GDP, revenues increased by 7 percent in Ivory Coast, nearly 4 percentage points in Kenya, nearly 3 percentage points in Cameroon, and 1 percentage point in Costa Rica. Most of the revenue increases were due to import duties, domestic sales taxes, and income taxes that arose from the general economic buoyancy stimulated by the coffee boom. Colombia and Costa Rica had modest coffee export taxes, and Cameroon and Ivory Coast taxed coffee (and cocoa) through their stabilization agencies.

In four of the five countries government revenues grew more rapidly than expenditures, so budget deficits declined or even became surpluses, reversing the process when coffee prices declined. Costa Rica was the exception: expenditures outpaced the steeply increasing revenues, and the budget deficit swelled from 2.2 percent of GDP in 1975 to 5.0 percent in 1978. Under the administration of José Figueres, elected in 1970, the government took a more active role in development and established a public holding company, CODESA, to engage in real investment and to take over ailing private enterprises with a view to reviving them. The government also increased social expenditure. Although these programs antedated the coffee boom, there is little doubt that the boom provided them with vital financial support.

Ivory Coast had also launched an ambitious public investment program in 1974–75, before the coffee boom, but in that case the boom provided the bulk of the financing as well as permitted some reduction in the budget deficit during the years of high coffee prices. An investment boom also took place in Cameroon, but in this case the focus was on projects related to recently discovered oil and were not financed by the coffee boom.

Thus the investment increases in Cameroon, Costa Rica, and Ivory Coast were by and large unrelated to the coffee boom, although in the latter two cases the coffee boom no doubt helped prolong the investment surge, and in the case of Costa Rica a large part of the increased revenues went into additional public consumption. In Kenya, investment increased by nearly 5 percentage points of GDP, no doubt as a result of escalating tea and especially coffee prices, but it went mainly into the private sector. And in Colombia the private sector consumed most of the increased income, although national savings also rose by virtue of a reduction in the budget deficit (by 2.3 percentage points of GDP), manifested in part as a fivefold increase in international reserves.

How can this experience under the coffee boom be summarized? Although the economic structure and the commodity boom were similar, these five countries responded in quite different ways. Cameroon dampened the boom at the start, limiting its impact on the economy by preventing farmers from receiving the higher prices and by running a conservative fiscal policy, although supporting a modest increase in investment. These measures moderated the impact on economic growth, the money supply, and inflation. Ivory Coast pursued a similar policy with respect to cocoa and coffee prices, with the government absorbing the bulk of the price increases. But Ivory Coast had already launched an ambitious public investment program that probably would have been difficult to finance fully, as it proved later, in the absence of the cocoa and coffee price boom, so the external events permitted expenditures that were planned in advance but that could not have taken place without the boom. In this indirect sense, the price increase was expansionary, even though it was handled conservatively from a fiscal point of view.

Colombia passed on most of the price increases to coffee growers and so allowed the increased revenues to enter the income stream, but the government then pursued a monetary and fiscal policy designed to stabilize the economy. The budget moved into surplus, and credit was tightened. Real money growth was substantially lower than in the other countries. When coffee prices fell, Colombia, now under a new administration, attempted to compensate for the loss of income by easing monetary and fiscal policies. In short, it pursued a stabilizing macroeconomic policy, with some success. But it incurred higher public debt at the end of the process than it would have if it had taxed more of the initial increase in coffee income.

Costa Rica, like Colombia, passed the price increases largely into private hands; but, like Ivory Coast, it had a government spending boom already in progress and used its increased tax revenues to finance part of the expenditure, borrowing abroad to cover the remainder. What is puzzling about Costa Rica is why it did not have a bigger boom and a greater inflation rate.

Part of the increased earnings went into private savings (without much increase in real investment) and thus helped improve the current account by 3 percent of GDP, despite a 2.8 percent deterioration in the budget deficit. And the low recorded inflation rate reflects the presence of price controls and subsidies on important consumer products. Inflation accelerated sharply in the next few years, but whatever effect the coffee boom had in this regard is confounded by the 1979–80 increase oil prices and in world interest rates, both of which hit Costa Rica hard, and by a steep currency devaluation in 1981.

Kenya passed virtually all of the coffee price increase on to growers in a deliberate act that in turn generated a boom in private investment. As revenues flowed into the government from the buoyant economy, budgetary control over expenditures weakened, and government consumption and transfers mushroomed. Fiscal discipline also suffered in Costa Rica, especially through the state agency CODESA.

From a macroeconomic perspective, Ivory Coast and Kenya apparently used their temporary windfall gains sensibly, by investing them, although in the former case the funds went into public investment of doubtful efficiency. Cameroon stabilized the economic effects of the coffee boom by sequestering the earnings abroad (although the full amounts do not appear as official reserves), as it did later with increased oil export earnings. Colombia allowed a great deal of the increased coffee earnings to enter the private income stream but then introduced tight monetary and fiscal actions to limit the short-run stimulus to the economy. This strategy was difficult to pursue and might have been more successful if a greater percentage of the coffee earnings had been kept out of the income stream, for example, through larger exactions by the National Coffee Fund or higher export taxes. Costa Rica consumed most of the increase, a move that would have made more sense had it been plausible to consider the high coffee prices permanent, which, however, was not the case.

In the event, Costa Rica, Ivory Coast, and Kenya all ran into serious financial difficulty after the oil shock and the subsequent recession, in part because their governments were by then spending at levels that could not be sustained by the prevailing tax system or further borrowing from abroad. Costa Rica's financial crisis hit in early 1981, before the recession and the general debt crisis. Cameroon and Colombia weathered this period with less difficulty, no doubt because they were net oil exporters; their problems came later.

It is now well known that a strong export boom (a similar analysis holds for an inflow of foreign aid or foreign investment, unless they finance only imports) may nurture what economists have come to call the Dutch disease.[11] A sharp rise in export receipts, unless sequestered abroad, will increase domestic incomes and domestic expenditures on both tradable and nontradable goods and services. Tradable goods and services can be provided from abroad—or from the domestic output of export- and import-competing goods—at relatively unchanged prices if the country does not alter its exchange rate or tariff structure and if the rest of the world is not experiencing inflation. In short, tradable goods can be supplied elastically from the rest of the world.

But nontradable goods and services must be provided out of local production. Thus their prices are bid up to attract labor and capital into their production and to help limit the growth in their consumption. That effect in turn draws resources away from the tradable goods sector (apart from the export product whose price has risen), and exports (other than the booming product) will fall, while imports rise. An export boom therefore has the paradoxical effect of depressing economic activity in nonbooming sectors that are subject to foreign competition, that is, most agriculture and manufacturing.[12]

These effects were strongly felt in Nigeria, whose once-diversified commodity exports all but disappeared in the presence of the oil boom and whose imports of foodstuffs displaced much domestic production, depressing agricultural production and driving people into the thriving cities in search of work, largely in construction and urban services. The pattern was somewhat the same in Mexico in the late 1970s, although Mexico's economy was better protected, so that some tradable goods were analytically like nontradables and enjoyed the spillover effects of the oil boom. The volume of non-oil exports stagnated between 1977 and 1981. Indonesia, as we have seen, preemptively devalued its currency in 1978, before the second oil price increase, to restore the price competitiveness of its traditional exports, mostly agricultural products.

Nonbeverage exports of the five coffee countries did not appear to decline markedly, but imports rose more rapidly than output in all five. In Colombia, Costa Rica, and Kenya, this was partly the result of import liberalization, which suggests that incremental demand for tradable goods was supplied from abroad. Perhaps nonbeverage exports were less affected because the boom was limited to just a few years.[13]

Economic Retrenchment in Theory and Practice

By late 1982 many of the countries in our sample found themselves facing a crisis of rather large proportions. The measures they employed to deal with the problem varied from country to country. To understand the behavior and performance of our countries in the 1980s and the role of the IMF in their recovery, it is necessary to digress for an analysis of economic retrenchment.

Analysis of Economic Retrenchment

A country that runs a deficit in its current account and borrows from abroad (or runs down its reserves) to finance the deficit is spending more than it is producing. If its external financing then dwindles, the country must cut its expenditures relative to its production (except for the limited period during which it can draw down any claims it may have against the rest of the world). The least painful way to reduce this gap is to increase output; but if that were easily done, it would likely have been done already, as countries do not willingly forgo output while borrowing to cover their expenditures. But the possibility must at least be allowed. Usually, however, countries are forced to cut their expenditures. This retrenchment is all the more difficult if the country's terms of trade have worsened, so that it must export more to cover a given volume of imports. Now expenditures cannot be met for two reasons: the lost financing plus the loss of production, in the sense that more production must go toward covering the imports that remain. For small countries, these losses are unavoidable, except insofar as the international community cushions them in some way, usually through official lending with some form of capital aid (such as loans from the World Bank) or temporary balance-of-payments support (such as loans from the International Monetary Fund). But in trying to reduce expenditures on imports, countries find that some of the reduction invariably spreads to domestically consumed goods and services. As a result, the output of those goods and services declines. Because the economy is unable to switch the labor and capital released by that reduction to production for export (or import substitutes) smoothly and quickly, it suffers yet another loss. This kind of double loss in output became a widespread phenomenon in Latin America and Africa during the 1980s.

This loss is in turn closely related to the structure of output and demand in the economy, which is influenced by past efforts the country may have made to reduce imports or to develop export markets. A country that has pursued a policy of import substitution over the long term will typically find that its ratio of imports to total output is lower than is the case for other countries and that the composition of imports is geared directly to the productive structure of the economy. That is, its imports comprise mainly essential materials and intermediate products, spare parts for foreign-made capital equipment, capital goods, and perhaps some basic foodstuffs. These imports cannot be squeezed without directly harming food consumption, industrial production, or investment. Not surprisingly, countries generally choose first to compress investment when they run into balance-of-payments difficulties. Imports of spare parts are delayed, and that reduces industrial and perhaps also agricultural production. Inventories are drawn down, and imports of materials needed for production may be delayed to save foreign exchange. Consequently, production also declines.

To avoid or reduce these costs, the country must increase its production for export, as it is generally less costly to earn foreign exchange under these circumstances than to save foreign exchange by compressing output. To that end, a country may introduce export incentives—the most common and general kind being a currency depreciation—to make production for export more profitable in local currency. But that will work only insofar as production for export can respond to the incentives, and that in turn depends on the nature of the country's export possibilities and on the flexibility of the economy, particularly its ability to move resources into export production. Many export products have gestation periods measured in years, insofar as trees have to be planted or factories built before a country is even in a position to increase supply substantially. Usually, however, some increase can be achieved through better care and more intense harvesting (for example, in the case of tree crops such as coffee) or more intensive and careful use of existing industrial plant (for example, with the help of quality control). Moreover, goods that have been smuggled out are encouraged to revert to legal channels.

By the time a crisis hits, however, it is too late to build flexibility into the economy; the authorities must make the best of whatever flexibility they have, and that depends largely on past policies. If a country has pursued only modestly protectionist policies, for instance, a relatively modest depreciation of the currency may make it profitable to export some goods that had been destined for the domestic market. If, in contrast, the protection against import competition has been extremely high, such that domestic production costs are far out of line with world prices, the currency will have to be depreciated considerably to generate new export products, and that will have undesirable side effects: the possibility of inflation may increase, and the local currency cost of servicing external debt will be greater.

The relationship between expenditure, terms of trade, and output is described more formally in the appendix to this chapter. Briefly, a decline in foreign lending to a country will require it to reduce its level of public and private consumption and investment, in terms of imported goods and services. That is inevitable. In addition, however, it will generally leave the country consuming more nontradable goods and services than it wants under the new circumstances, so its government and citizens will want to reallocate factors of production from nontradables to export and import-competing goods, so as to restore some of its earlier consumption of imports. Such reallocation cannot always be accomplished smoothly or costlessly; labor and capital released from the nontradable sector may not find immediate employment in the export or import-competing sectors. How smoothly the reallocation occurs depends not only on technology in the export sector relative to the nontradable sector, but also on the flexibility of factor prices and the mobility of factors of production. In the best of circumstances (easily movable factors, flexible factor prices), the country will shift resources smoothly, with little loss in total production. In the worst of circumstances, labor and capital will become idle in the nontradable sector and will not be absorbed in the export sector. In these circumstances, the country must cut its absorption (consumption plus investment) of imports by the entire loss in capital inflow, and in addition will have a loss in absorption of nontradables as well, due to a decline in demand for them. If in addition the country's terms of trade have worsened, there is a still further need to reduce absorption of imports because the country's exports will purchase fewer imports.

Three further points should be noted. The first is that net resource inflows lead to a larger-than-otherwise production (and consumption) of nontradable goods. In other words, a net capital inflow at least indirectly finances nontradable production, even when it is allocated to the export sector, by virtue of the fact that it pushes up the relative price of nontradables. In this respect, the effect of capital inflows resembles that of an export boom—that is, both are a brand of Dutch disease, discussed in chapter 1.

Second, *any* reallocation of resources from an initially optimal point will lead to a recorded decline in the output of the economy when measured at the prices that prevailed at the initial point. This will be true even when the country is better off with a different allocation of resources owing to the changed circumstances. In other words, the real GDP that is typically measured does not always adequately indicate the change in the well-being of a country due to unavoidably changed circumstances.[1]

Note, too, that if our country has been importing capital from the rest of the world and if that capital has been used efficiently, it has permitted an increase in our national production. Provided the yield on that investment exceeds the cost of servicing the debt, our country is better off than it would otherwise be even if the net resource inflow has turned *negative*, that is, even if debt-service obligations exceed new capital inflows. This point is often forgotten in discussions of resource flows and external debt. Of course, our country would be still better off in this period if it could avoid the payment on the outstanding debt, but that would presumably involve costs in subsequent periods. A special problem can arise, however, when past debts have been incurred to invest in nontradable goods, such as housing or electricity generation for domestic consumption. The need to shift resources out of nontradables following a sharp decline in net resource inflows will lower the rate of return on investments in that sector. Unless the risks of variable returns have been shared with the creditors, which is typically not the case on non-equity investment, the debtor country may have to service the external debt at a rate not covered by the now lower returns on the original investments. (By the same token, however, rates of return are now higher on investments in export goods, and all of that increase accrues to the domestic owners if the external debt service is fixed.)

A rough idea of the total impact on any country resulting from an adverse movement in the terms of trade (where such movement occurred), a decline in net resource inflows, and a decline in production of nontradables can be obtained by manipulating the national accounts identity and then trying to measure the components. For any country,

$$E = GDP - rD - X + M, \tag{1}$$

where E is the total expenditure in the country during some period of time (usually a year), X is exports, M is imports (exclusive of debt service), rD is the payment on the external debt D, and GDP is the country's gross domestic product, all measured in current prices. We can then measure everything in terms of import goods by deflating by the price of imports:

$$E = NP + M = NP + XT + dD - rD, \tag{2}$$

where N is the volume of nontraded goods produced and consumed, X is the volume of exports, P is the price of nontraded goods in terms of imported goods, T is the price of exports in terms of imports (the international terms of trade), and E is the value of total expenditure measured in terms of imported goods.[2] D is the value of net external debt in terms of imported goods, r is the yield on external debt, and dD indicates the change in external debt as measured by the current account balance, such that $M = X + dD - rD$, and dD − rD measures the net inflow of resources. We can then decompose equation (2) into two parts. The terms N, X, and P, roughly speaking, are determined by internal factors. P is sometimes confusingly called the real exchange rate in the economic literature, although it bears only a rough relationship to measurements that carry the same label; it is the relative price between nontraded goods and imports. The terms T, dD, and r, roughly speaking, are determined by the external environment, although of course for any particular country dD and the risk premium embedded in r are influenced by the country's policies and prospects. Furthermore, dD is the *net* change in debt, after taking into account the repayments on foreign debt and the capital outflow from the country in question. With short maturities or with private capital outflow, dD could become strongly negative. Private capital outflow is of course heavily influenced by domestic considerations. In addition, many developing countries may influence their terms of trade, T, in the short run, because world markets are not perfect even for commodities, and some developing countries are dominant suppliers of their export commodities.

Absorption *(E) must* decline when a country experiences a worsening in its terms of trade and loses its sources of external financing, unless new sources of credit can be found. The key policy issue in these circumstances is whether resource reallocation can take place smoothly, with a minimal loss of output and employment. The difficulty of adjustment in the short run is measured by the decline in absorption, not by the decline in output. The compression that must take place in imports is especially important in many countries. By that measure, difficulties varied greatly among our countries over the period from 1978 (just before OPEC II) to 1983 (after the Mexican debt crisis), from a decline of 55 percent in Kenya (where imports were atypically high in 1978, made possible by the coffee boom) to an increase of 74 percent in India (see table 2.1).[3] Domestic production fell in Brazil, Chile, Costa Rica, and Nigeria.

Table 2.1
Import compression

	Changes in 1975 imports (in 1973 prices) as a percent of 1973 imports	Changes in 1983 imports (in 1978 prices) as a percent of 1978 imports
Argentina[a]	37	-18
Brazil	19	-26*
Cameroon[a]	34	-11
Chile	-34*	-23*
Colombia	1	24
Costa Rica[a]	17	-41*
Cote d'Ivoire	6	-28
India	-11	74
Indonesia[a]	58	46
Kenya	-15	-55
Korea	29	17
Mexico[a]	32	-26
Morocco	49	-14
Nigeria[a]	146	-32*
Pakistan	24	37
Sri Lanka	-3	37
Thailand	-15	29
Turkey	35	49

*Production of nontraded goods declined.
a. U.S. producer prices used to deflate second-year imports.
Source: Author's calculation from IMF, *International Financial Statistics*, national accounts.

Financing Government

The required reduction in absorption applies to the country as a whole. Governments have an additional problem. The governments of developing countries usually spend more than they collect in revenues. The resulting deficits can be financed in three ways: by borrowing from the nonbank public, by borrowing from the rest of the world, or by borrowing from the banking system, including the central bank. The first source is relatively limited in developing countries because their domestic capital markets are poor or non-existent, although some countries—Brazil, Korea, Mexico, and Turkey, for instance—have raised significant sums from this source. Moreover, some governments on occasion have required households and nonbank institutions to purchase government bonds.[4]

A government can borrow abroad as long as it is creditworthy. The advantage of foreign loans is that, through imports, they provide additional resources to the economy for consumption or investment. Their disadvantage is that the government must service them out of its future revenues, which poses a potential problem because the debt is usually in foreign currency, whereas revenues are in the domestic currency (unless the government owns an important export activity, such as oil production). This distinction is unimportant for a mature economy, but as we shall see, it can be significant for many developing countries, where the ability of the government to raise additional revenues may be sharply limited.

Raising funds from the third source, the domestic banking system, will either increase the supply of money and other liquid assets (and thus contribute to inflation) or else will crowd out credit to private firms (and thus reduce private investment).

As noted earlier, most developing countries increased their foreign borrowing substantially following the two oil price increases. When commercial bank lending declined during the debt crisis, countries at first tried to find official sources of foreign funds. This proved to be difficult, in part because many export credit agencies were also worried about the deteriorating creditworthiness of the borrowers and in part because developing countries had already heavily exploited official sources of funds, which tend to carry lower interest rates and often longer maturities than commercial bank and other private loans.[5]

Extensive borrowing from the International Monetary Fund took place following both oil price increases and increased further when commercial bank loans became more difficult or even impossible to get. IMF credit outstanding to developing countries rose by SDR 27.4 billion (about $31 billion) between the end of 1980 and the end of 1984, the period in which the debt crisis was most acute. In addition, the World Bank in 1980 introduced structural adjustment loans (SALs), a form of quick-disbursing funds, to support policy reforms in various sectors of the economy, such as agriculture or energy.[6] World Bank lending increased from $5.8 billion in 1980 to $11.1 billion in 1985, of which $1.5 billion consisted of SALs. But funds from these two sources could not substitute on a continuing basis for private lending, and in any case the IMF funding was limited in amount and relatively short in maturity. Table 2.2 reports new IMF standby agreements in our eighteen countries, averaging 4.6 a year over the period 1973–88, with nine countries reaching standby agreements in 1983, the peak year. Table 2.3 presents annual net disbursements from the highly concessional International Development Association (IDA) and the World Bank over this period, and total outstanding credits (so changes between years represent net new funds) from the IMF, including those from the Oil Facility and the Compensatory Financing Facility as well as those issued under standby agreements.

When external funding began to dry up, governments were forced to reduce their deficits or to finance them from the domestic banking system. Cutting expenditures, especially those to which the public has become accustomed or thinks it is entitled on the basis of past pronouncements by government officials, is politically difficult, as is raising taxes, and collecting additional revenues is not always administratively feasible. Deficit reductions therefore tend to concentrate in the first instance on postponing planned investment expenditure or stretching out expenditure on projects already begun. But the inability of governments to respond quickly, combined with some hope that the adverse external situation will be temporary, typically leads governments to shift their financial requirements to the banking system. And this move typically turns out to be inflationary.

One of the sovereign attributes of government is to create money for the country's residents.[7] Since the cost of producing modern money, largely bank notes, is less than the face value, the issuing agency makes a profit, called seigniorage, on new money. This profit is typically turned over to the government as revenue, although occasionally it is used to make subsidized loans to state or private enterprises or to purchase nonperforming assets from the deposit-taking banks to improve their capital positions; the latter practice became especially common following the numerous domestic financial crises that occurred in developing countries in 1982–83.

Inflation erodes the value, measured in command over goods and services, of all assets that are denominated in nominal terms. If further inflation is expected, purchasers of the assets can insist on a higher interest rate to compensate for this loss in value, or they can require that the asset be indexed to protect them against future variations in the rate of inflation. But these forms of hedging against inflation do not work for currency. Following an unexpected price increase, such as that produced by the two oil shocks, the public will want to increase its currency holdings. That process generates additional seigniorage. If the rate of inflation is higher than the public expects, it will attempt to economize on the use of currency, but thereafter will want to replenish its holdings continually in order to maintain some relationship with the growth in its expenditures. The portion of the seigniorage that is due to this additional, inflation-driven demand for currency is known as the "inflation tax."[8]

Table 2.2
Standby arrangements with the IMF (eighteen countries)

Country	1973	1974	1975	1976	1977	1978	1979
Argentina				8/260	9/159.5		
Brazil							
Cameroon							
Chile		1/79	3/79				
Colombia	6/20						
Costa Rica				7/11.6			
Cote d'Ivoire							
India							
Indonesia	5/50						
Kenya			7/67.2 (3yr Eff)			11/17.25	8/122.4 canc10/8
Korea	4/20 (8 Mth)	5/20 (7 Mth)	10/20 (8 Mth)		5/20 (7 Mth)		
Mexico					1/518 (3yr Eff)		
Morocco							
Nigeria							
Pakistan	8/75	11/75			3/80	3/80	
Sri Lanka		4/24.5			12/93		1/260.3 (3yr Eff)
Thailand						7/42.25	
Turkey						4/300 4/3360 (9 Mth)	7/250 canc6/80

Source: IMF *Annual Reports*, 1971 to 1989. Notes: Amount in million SDRs follows month in which standby became effective; canc = canceled in indicated month; Eff = Extended Fund Facility, a three-year program (original term in parentheses).

1980	1981	1982	1983	1984	1985	1986	1987	1988
			1/1500 canc 1/84	12/1182.			7/947.5 (14 mth)	
			3/4239. (3 yr Eff)					8/109 (18Mth) 9/69 (6Mth)
			1/500		8/825 (3yr Eff)			
3/60.5 (2 Yrs)	3/276.7 (3yr Eff) canc12/8	12/92.25			3/54		10/40 (19 Mth)	
	2/484.5 (3yr Eff)			8/82.75 (9 Mth)	6/66.2	6/100 (2 Yrs) canc 2/88		2/94 (14 Mth)
	11/5000 (3yr Eff) canc 5/84							
8/241.5 (2 yrs) canc 1/82		1/151.5	3/175.9 (18 Mth)		2/85.2			2/85 (18 Mth)
3/640 canc 2/81	2/576		7/575.8 (18 Mth)		7/280 (18 Mth)			
	1/3611. (3yr Ear)		1/3410. (3yr Eff)			11/1400 (18 Mth)		
10/810 (3yr Eff) canc3/81	3/817.0 (19 Mth) canc4/82	4/281.2	9/300 (18 Mth)		9/200 (18 Mth) canc12/86	12/230 (16 Mth)		8/210 (16 Mth)
							1/650	
11/1268 (3yr Eff) canc12/8	12/919 (3yr Eff)							12/273 (15 Mth)
			9/100 (10 Mth)					
	6/814.5	11/271.5			6/400 (21 Mth)			
6/1250 (3yr Eff)			7/225 canc 4/84	4/225				

Table 2.3
IMF credit outstanding and World Bank loans, 1973–1988

		1973	1974	1975	1976	1977	1978	1979	1980	1981	1982	1983	1984	1985	1986	1987	1988
Argentina	IMF	174	64	250	456	345	0	0	0	0	0	1121	1121	2105	2241	2716	2733
Brazil	WBL	84	26	35	0	13	51	33	31	0	36	11	0	34	282	487	766
	IMF	0	0	0	0	0	0	0	0	0	499	2526	4270	4205	3680	2803	2477
Cameroon	WBL	235	159	244	137	236	343	311	287	0	172	531	878	444	1885	1878	361
	IMF	0	5	12	34	34	33	25	12	3	1	0	0	0	0	0	70
	IDA	10	8	11	15	22	17	19	17	25	87	0	0	0	1	1	0
	SAL	10	6	17	10	8	35	37	29	0	3	28	24	20	134	97	36
Chile	IMF	79	160	331	402	301	266	136	96	42	6	579	795	991	1088	1032	983
	IDA	2	0	0	0	0	0	0	0	0	0	0	0	0	0	0	0
	WBL	21	0	0	4	9	27	21	5	0	10	8	10	33	464	414	257
	SAL													250	250	250	
Colombia	IMF	0	0	0	0	0	0	0	0	0	0	0	0	0	0	0	0
	IDA	2	0	0	0	0	0	0	0	0	0	0	0	0	0	0	0
	WBL	129	29	95	11	51	101	85	142	0	107	202	74	345	1166	571	337
Costa Rica	IMF	0	19	11	29	24	31	44	45	88	84	183	159	172	141	93	53
	WBL													6	178	42	0
	SAL													80			
Cote d'Ivoire	IMF	19	8	11	11	25	31	0	0	319	435	589	603	566	509	407	369
	IDA	0	0	0	0	0	0	0	0	0	0	0	0	0	0	0	0
	WBL	13	9	26	18	25	50	74	54	18	76	159	142	108	351	329	205
	SAL									150		251				250	
India	IMF	0	497	698	406	125	0	0	266	566	2066	3533	4000	3825	3494	2856	2069
	IDA	386	327	433	509	496	311	364	547	759	945	970	637	518	1401	1081	790
	WBL	57	0	0	0	48	135	109	102	0	332	211	318	62	868	1043	967
	SAL										0	251	421	42	42	505	463
Indonesia	IMF	19	66	86	115	76	36	0	35	44	343	0	0	0	0	0	0
	IDA	53	0	0	0	0	0	30	0	111	291	429	500	1225	898	1585	1106
	WBL	0	32	69	125	182	216	191	252	175	310	398	388	442	352	269	304
Kenya	IMF	0	9	9	11	48	52	108	17	68	279	103	0	0	0	56	0
	IDA	19	9	9	11	13	18	22	17	68	0	0	0	0	105	0	129

Country		24	13	24	75	37	67	62	46	0	30	84	89	66	247	133	0
Korea	WBL	0	110	217	302	280	202	104	535	1071	1142	1293	1599	1373	1266	370	0
	SAL	9	13	18	13	11	6	0	0	0	0	0	0	0	0	0	0
	IMF	69	58	96	212	298	311	374	363	0	313	421	277	177	1068	419	0
	IDA	0	0	0	319	419	229	103	0	0	201	1204	2408	2703	3319	3639	3570
Mexico	WBL	138	88	184	99	177	266	248	360	0	201	206	169	336	1476	1435	607
	IMF	0	0	0	115	115	173	151	248	387	788	879	1011	1083	839	755	696
	IDA	7	9	2	3	4	1	1	1	1	12	0	0	0	0	0	0
	WBL	22	33	84	62	19	100	93	100	0	46	136	104	88	640	513	227
Morocco																	200
	IMF	0	0	0	0	0	0	0	0	0	0	0	0	0	0	0	0
	IDA	7	4	2	14	1	1	73	48	0	52	122	185	102	625	886	75
Nigeria	WBL	42	17	38	440	60	83	337	300	650	1057	1317	1266	1116	847	567	370
	IDA	130	239	374	35	438	395	73	71	69	710	208	140	209	327	238	212
	WBL	89	22	6	27	91	48	43	0	0	60	36	0	0	154	232	195
Pakistan		38	0	0		43	35										
	IMF	74	102	125	134	170	186	234	211	347	341	331	328	292	234	165	209
	IDA	5	8	18	4	9	12	7	20	23	479	20	42	62	136	95	184
	WBL	5	1	3	0	0	2	1	0	0	0	3	20	0	16	10	3
Sri Lanka	IMF	0	0	0	67	67	136	182	143	606	636	867	807	929	808	645	474
	IDA	0	0	2	4	9	6	5	3	10	82	10	0	0	0	0	0
	WBL	57	8	31	15	47	112	119	151	90	292	297	200	156	759	343	0
Thailand											150	176					
	IMF	0	0	208	337	337	478	480	827	1136	1319	1497	1455	1208	887	543	222
	IDA	13	12	13	15	24	10	5	0	0	0	0	0	0	0	0	0
Turkey	WBL	50	54	82	86	109	193	255	209	102	–81	815	228	487	1448	1004	742
	SAL									375	305	301	376				
Totals to all	IMF	1027	3740	7435	12608	13078	10277	7976	8486	13367	19310	29899	34905	35180	33417	29237	25543
countries	IDA	786	704	1014	1231	1276	1033	1196	1374	1838	1324	2900	2538	2440	5595	4842	4649
	WBL	1816	816	1699	1338	2197	3635	3515	3801	–717	3210	4580	4093	3542	19681	14728	6000
$/SDR		1.21	1.22	1.17	1.16	1.21	1.30	1.32	1.28	1.16	1.10	1.05	0.98	1.10	1.22	1.42	1.35

Source: World Bank, *Annual Report*, summary statement of loans, IBRD financial statement; the amount of structural adjustment loans is given below the World Bank total. IDA is development credits, International Development Association, in millions of $U.S. (disbursed portion of loans only, calculated from outstanding loans, receipts net of any repayments). IMF credits outstanding are use of Fund credit, General Department, in millions of SDRs.

It has been said that inflation is the cruelest tax of all. That may sound poetic, but it does not make economic sense. Although it is not respectable to say so, the inflation tax is in fact quite an efficient tax, at least up to a point, and not obviously an inequitable one. If inflation arises because of an unexpected price increase and looks as though it will return to its previous rate, then the inflation tax comes close to that will-o'-the-wisp of all public finance specialists, a lump-sum tax. It gains revenue, in the form of additional seigniorage, without affecting the behavior of economic agents on any margin. If the inflation is expected to continue, the public will reduce its real money holdings somewhat, thus bearing some inconvenience, but then will continue to increase money holdings in line with expenditures, thus augmenting the government's revenue. The demand for currency turns out to be quite inelastic. In economies with a poorly developed financial sector, currency has few substitutes. At moderate rates of inflation, people apparently prefer to endure the inflation tax than to alter radically their behavior so as to avoid it. The result can be consequential for the government. If the ratio of currency to GDP is 10 percent, typical of developing countries, and inflation is 20 percent, the inflation tax generates revenue of 2 percent of GDP, or about 10 percent of government revenues.

Of course, at sufficiently high rates of inflation the erosion in currency value is great enough to induce substantial changes in behavior. People will try to spend their currency as soon as they receive it, thus paradoxically increasing the rate of inflation. The distortions to economic behavior become substantial. Or they will seek an alternative liquid asset for their transactions. Most often this is foreign currency, and it gives rise to the "dollarization" of a high-inflation economy.[9] At sufficiently high rates of inflation, economies in the use of domestic currency become so great that the inflation tax declines as inflation increases further. But the provocation must be extreme, because it is very inconvenient not to use currency. Experience suggests that the inflation tax rises with the rate of inflation until the latter is well over 100 percent a year, although no governments have endured inflation at those rates long enough to discover whether the tax would decline; they have ample other reasons for wanting to bring down the inflation rate.

It may be asked why people do not switch more quickly to a foreign currency. The criminalization of dealings in foreign currency may inhibit it. But it can also be expensive, especially if currency controls give rise to a black-market rate of exchange greatly depreciated from the official rate. Moreover, although holding foreign currency as a liquid store of value is a private matter, using it for local transactions is a collective matter. Without a collective decision to sanction such use, it is likely to take place only under extreme provocation such as hyperinflation (defined as inflation in excess of 1,000 percent a year).

It is often said that the inflation tax is highly regressive, falling disproportionately on the poor. In fact, we know little about the distributional consequences of the inflation tax, but it is highly unlikely that the tax is regressive. It is probably true, but irrelevant, that a much higher fraction of the assets of poor people is held as currency than is true for the rich. For a variety of reasons, the rich can diversify their assets more easily than the poor can. But I would conjecture that the rich in developing countries hold a higher ratio of currency to income than do the poor, even in countries with moderately high inflation.[10] The poor live from hand to mouth, partly on credit from shopkeepers, and they are likely to hold their cash earnings only for relatively short periods. The rich in developing countries carry ready cash continuously for transactions purposes, since alternative means of payment are poorly developed. If this conjecture is correct, then a tax on currency is progressive in the usual sense of the term, namely, in the sense that those with higher incomes pay a higher rate of tax on their incomes. Moreover, an inflation tax falls also on many illegal and otherwise tax-evading activities, and in that respect also it can be considered progressive.

This argument should not be overplayed. Over time, as noted above, high rates of inflation can lead to economies in the use of currency and in bank balances that do not bear interest and thus will erode the base against which an inflation tax can be levied. In addition, accelerating inflation, or highly variable rates of inflation, can distort investment and consumption decisions in ways that impose substantial costs on society. Accelerating inflation suggests that the overall management of the economy is undisciplined and perhaps out of control, whereas variable rates of inflation introduce a source of uncertainty that greatly complicates long-term planning of any kind, including investment decisions crucial to future growth. The point here is simply that, in harping on the many disadvantages of inflation, we should not forget that steady, moderate inflation represents a form of taxation that is quite efficient when compared with alternative methods of raising revenue in developing countries.

Most developing countries were already taking advantage of the inflation tax in the 1970s. The average rate of inflation in those countries, measured by the consumer price index (often only in the capital city), over the period 1972–82 was 21 percent a year. After the debt crisis, it rose to 40 percent a year during the period 1982–87, although this figure reflects more the sharp increase in inflation in a relatively few countries, most of them in Latin America, than a general increase in inflation in all developing countries. A number of governments, largely inadvertently, substituted inflation for foreign financing. Unlike foreign financing, borrowing from the banking system does not make additional resources available to the economy; it can only reallocate the existing output. If the government's claim on that output through its budget does not diminish, something else must give way, and that is some combination of private investment and consumption brought about by the reduced real spending necessary to replenish the real value of currency holdings.[11] So the increased inflation of the 1980s is intimately related to the debt crisis.

The assumption in conventional, largely frictionless economic analysis is that a still-solvent borrowing country could continue to attract funds from abroad by being willing to pay a somewhat higher interest rate. At a minimum, the experience of the 1980s should raise questions about this assumption.

After the debt crisis many banks were unwilling to lend to certain developing countries at all and desired to liquidate their loans as soon as possible. Various institutional reasons explain why the banks behaved in this way, after having been so eager to lend with little question shortly before. But there is also one systemic reason, namely that the future prospects of a loan by any one bank depend on the ability of the country to continue to get loans from other banks. Countries (like growing firms) do not have to pay down their indebtedness; they typically repay each loan by incurring new ones. It is the ability to borrow afresh that determines creditworthiness, not the ability to reduce total outstanding debt. A country's ability to invest productively depends on its ability to attract a net inflow of resources. Once some banks pulled back, this action increased the (valid) incentive to others to do so as well, since legitimate questions could then be raised about the ability of the country to continue servicing its external debts in the short run (see Sachs 1984; and Cooper and Sachs 1985).

The same could be said for nonbank lenders. Once a country's ability to service its debts comes into question, it will be questioned by all potential creditors, not just by banks. But that argument just applies to foreign currency loans. Surely, it may be argued, at sufficiently high real domestic interest rates some foreigners would be willing to lend to the country and bear the exchange risk, if necessary reinvesting in the country until such time as it is profitable to repatriate the investment.

That argument presumes a degree of specialized knowledge about the country that probably provides the foundation for the comparative advantage of banks as lending institutions. But here another obstacle comes into play. The interest rates required to attract foreign or domestic capital to buy government securities may be so high that they will jeopardize the basic financial structure of the country.

Any system of credit, however finely articulated institutionally, operates by borrowing from depositors on demand or over the short term and by lending to businesses over the longer term. Thus financial institutions as a group carry a maturity risk. Their lending and borrowing contracts presumably cover possible adverse contingencies that lie within the realm of recent experience. But they never cover all possible contingencies, particularly not a rise in real interest rates that falls way outside historical experience. Such a rise is precisely what happened in a number of countries: interest rates shot up in response to the reduction of foreign funds. This increase, combined with the world recession and declining terms of trade for many developing countries, rendered nonviable many business loans in which the interest rate risk was borne by the borrower; the increase was equally disastrous for some financial institutions in which the risk was borne by the lender.[12] The result was a series of domestic financial crises in 1982–83, which were particularly severe in Chile, Costa Rica, Korea, Mexico, and Turkey. Some of the crises involved shaky operators and fraud. But the fundamental cause of the crisis in each case was that the financial structure had become so fragile that it could not handle a significant disturbance, which at other times would have been considered an isolated event.[13]

The domestic financial crises created a further dilemma for the monetary authorities. Reducing absorption called for tighter credit and high real interest rates, but such action would have exacerbated the circumstances that precipitated the financial crises and could have invited a complete collapse of the domestic financial system, something that policymakers cannot seriously contemplate in any modern economy. So the monetary authorities had to walk a tightrope, encouraging disabsorption while still preserving (often through direct financial support form the central bank) the large financial institutions and even ensuring that some of their major clients would not go under. Currency devaluation, which meant raising the local currency debt service on foreign loans, was often a precipitating or an aggravating event. Yet currency depreciation was an all-but-universal prescription for minimizing the loss in output in a period of disabsorption. Indeed, it was widely encouraged or even required by the IMF when that institution was asked for financial support.

The Role of the International Monetary Fund

The International Monetary Fund, established in 1946, operates on a set of principles that pertain to the financial relationship between its members and the rest of the international community. One principle it adhered to in the early years was the fixity of exchange rates, which were to be changed only through international agreement. But that commitment was formally altered in 1978 to allow a variety of exchange rate arrangements, provided they were not manipulated "to prevent effective balance-of-payments adjustment or to gain an unfair competitive advantage over other members" and provided members "take into account in their intervention policies the interests of other members" (Article IV). The IMF principles do not address trade policy as such, but they do require that member countries keep their currencies convertible for current account transactions (that is, trade in goods and services), unless restrictions are required temporarily for balance-of-payments reasons. The IMF also has the capacity to lend to members for limited periods of time to help them get over their balance-of-payments difficulties.

To qualify for loans beyond a certain level, the borrowing country must prepare a "letter of intent" indicating that it will pursue certain policy actions (agreed with the IMF) that are designed to reestablish balance-of-payments equilibrium within a few years. Since all members are committed to the principle of convertible currency, it is not surprising that the IMF defines the equilibrium to be achieved as one that, if possible, does *not* involve balance-of-payments restrictions on current transactions; indeed, it would be inappropriate to sanction continuing, indefinite use of such restrictions. A country that wishes to maintain such restrictions indefinitely should not have joined the IMF in the first place, or should withdraw (as Czechoslovakia did in 1949 and Cuba in 1960). In practice, however, many member countries maintain such restrictions under a "temporary" clause in the IMF articles and have done so for many years. So a compromise must be struck between the objective, to which all members formally adhere, and the reality, which makes it difficult for them to move to convertibility in the near future. Whereas the IMF pushes toward greater convertibility, some member countries resist it. That is often a source of tension between the IMF and some of its members, even though in recent years the IMF has probably not pressed as hard as it should on this point.

The decision to go to the IMF for assistance rests with the member country, which means that some countries go later than may be desirable and thus complicate the process of adjustment from an unsustainable payments position. The IMF may assist in drawing up the letter of intent. In any case, it must assure itself that the proposed program is both feasible and will accomplish the agreed objective. It then provides funds to permit a less drastic reduction in absorption than would otherwise be required. The loans are repayable in three to five years, and in up to ten years under the Extended Fund Facility, which covers three-year programs in more difficult cases. Although the loans carry below-market interest rates, they are meant to provide a temporary bridge to sustainability, not foreign aid.

In ensuring the restoration of a sustainable payments position, the IMF usually encourages countries to focus their reforms on four policy variables: their government's budget deficit; the rate at which domestic credit is created, which is closely related to the budget deficit when the local capital market is weak or nonexistent and when access to foreign credit is limited; the exchange rate; and interest rates, for both depositors and borrowers. After the second oil shock, the IMF also addressed domestic pricing policy for oil products, when those were badly out of line with world prices.

Ordinarily, a country comes to the IMF when it is drawing down reserves and has to cover an otherwise unsustainable payments deficit, however that problem arose. The country must therefore retrench, recognizing the implications already discussed. Its central concern will be to retrench as smoothly as possible, inasmuch as resources must be shifted from the nontradable to the tradable sectors of the economy. It must refrain from expanding domestic credit if it wishes to promote disabsorption. Provided high interest rates do not throttle the economy, they can both help ration credit and encourage households to place their savings in the financial system, where they can be mobilized for investment; moreover, they can help discourage the flight of capital, which is possible even in the presence of formal controls on capital outflows.

As we have already seen, a straightforward reduction in absorption is likely to entail a decline in total output unless wages are exceptionally flexible and labor and capital highly mobile. Currency depreciation is designed to make the export industries more profitable (and will have the same effect on import-competing industries if it has not already been achieved through import restrictions). The idea is to pull factors of production away from the nontradable sector or to employ hitherto unemployed labor. If successful, that will minimize the decline in total output in a setting in which the production of nontradables must decline, except in those rare cases when resources are so underutilized that the full excess of absorption can be eliminated through an increase in output. Import controls maintained for balance-of-payments reasons should, if possible, be reduced during the adjustment. Currency devaluation also contributes to that process, by providing a more favorable exchange rate to the import-competing industries, in exchange for some loss of protection achieved through the abolition of import controls. The IMF loan is to tide over the country between the currency devaluation and the increase in exports. Normally, the program is implemented in one year and takes effect over two to four years, but, as mentioned earlier, the IMF introduced the Extended Fund Facility in 1974 to make financing available for a three-year program designed to take effect over a total of ten years.

The IMF need not go beyond this policy framework. In practice, the IMF team is drawn into detailed discussions of exactly what expenditures should be cut or what taxes should be raised to reduce the budget deficit. That may be helpful as technical advice, but the program should not be conditioned on those details. Rather, the responsibility for meeting the targets of the letter of intent should be left solely with the officials of the country concerned. They should establish the recovery priorities within the macroeconomic framework worked out with the IMF, and in doing so will no doubt take political as well as economic considerations into account.

When it comes to the politically unpopular decisions required to reduce absorption, many officials would just as soon hand responsibility for the disagreeable actions over to the IMF, or at least hope to mobilize its support (beyond the overall targets) for the actions that finance ministers must persuade reluctant prime ministers or cabinets to take. Indeed, they have led many to believe that the IMF forces countries to take politically disagreeable and sometimes economically costly actions.[14] The IMF itself has abetted this damaging process by becoming unnecessarily involved in the details of each program, a practice reinforced by its formal cooperation with the World Bank since 1986 in drawing up a jointly agreed policy framework paper for some countries. This cooperation is designed to ensure that both institutions are proceeding within a consistent framework, rather than giving countries conflicting views (as sometimes occurred before, especially with respect to exchange rate policy).

A related problem has arisen in connection with inflation. There is no reason for the international community to be concerned about the rate of inflation in any particular developing country unless it represents a serious impediment to reestablishing payments equilibrium as defined by the IMF. If exchange rates are managed appropriately, a proper concern of the IMF, they can reconcile divergent rates of inflation among countries. Each country should be permitted to choose its own rate of inflation, unless by choice it chooses not to, for example, by tying its currency to that of another country and managing its monetary and fiscal actions accordingly. Experience has shown that a wide range of inflation rates is consistent with both economic growth and payments equilibrium. During the early 1980s, however, the IMF went on an anti-inflation crusade, in developing as well as developed countries. Since it can be costly to reduce inflation that has been built into the expectations and planning of households and firms, the IMF was drawn into policy recommendations that were even more controversial than those required to reduce absorption. It thereby incurred much displeasure and strayed from its proper international function. Nonetheless, it is easy to imagine how financial officials, desiring to reduce inflation for *domestic* reasons, might invoke the support and the authority of the IMF in persuading their governments and people to accept difficult actions that were likely to be costly in the short run. The IMF should draw a sharper distinction between technical assistance to financial officials with worthy objectives and conditions formally required to qualify for loans in support of balance-of-payments adjustment programs.

In putting together a quantitative framework for a sustainable payments position, the IMF must make projections of exports, imports, and capital movements and of the sensitivity of these flows to changes in policy. All such projections proceed from judgments that are grounded in analysis but nonetheless may be in error. Much of the disagreement between the IMF and national officials hinges on these judgments. The national official is typically more optimistic than Fund staff, because anticipated favorable developments imply that less difficult action will be required to restore equilibrium, although occasionally the roles are reversed.

When a country has incurred substantial external debt, the IMF must also decide (1) how to handle interest and amortization payments on that debt and (2) what size of new loans it can plausibly assume. During the post-1982 debt crisis the IMF strongly urged the commercial banks to make new loans to some indebted countries, in effect making the release of IMF funds contingent on agreement between the country and its bank creditors on rescheduling the outstanding debt and on the magnitude of new loans. This practice had the probably inadvertent consequence of strengthening the bargaining position of the creditor banks with respect to the terms of rescheduling. As a result, there was sometimes a long delay in launching an IMF-approved program. The IMF can hardly formally sanction continuing arrearage of interest and amortization payments, but in 1989 it ceased making the release of its funds contingent on agreement between the borrowing country and its commercial bank creditors. Instead, it simply assumed in its quantitative framework that certain private capital flows would be available, thus creating the option of a buildup of arrears if a new loan package could not be negotiated within a reasonable time.

Economists, whether at the IMF or elsewhere, tend to treat economic stabilization as a matter of meeting certain technical conditions (for example, with respect to the creation of domestic credit or the exchange rate) to ensure a successful outcome—on the assumption, of course, that external circumstances do not change for the worse. But in doing so they overlook the fact that such stabilization cannot be achieved unless the behavior of key economic agents in the private as well as in the public sector is altered. That behavior is likely to be altered only if the program has credibility, in two respects. First, it must be at least superficially coherent, without gross internal contradictions or omissions. Second, it is expected to endure for some period of time; that is, it will not be scuttled or drastically changed in the face of proximate difficulties, including public opposition.

If a depreciation of the currency is to improve the trade balance and maintain economic activity in the presence of contractionary fiscal and monetary policy, economic agents must be willing to reallocate resources, including investment funds, into the export and import-competing activities. They will be unwilling to do this if they believe the new policies are only temporary and that the increased profitability of exports will be quickly undermined by inflation uncompensated by further currency depreciation. Similarly, a decline in demand brought about by cuts in public expenditures, higher taxes, or tighter credit will presumably lead to a drop in the rate of inflation. But interest rates in auction or curb markets will drop only if the decline in inflation is expected to last. If not, real short-term interest rates will rise sharply, raising the real burden of financing the government (indeed, all debtors), thus possibly undermining the new fiscal program. What might otherwise be a relatively smooth transition may be converted into a sharp economic downturn via the bankruptcy of business firms and even financial institutions. Expectations about success will also influence the extent to which resident capital returns from abroad, thus augmenting reserves, and the extent to which import liberalization (through the substitution of currency depreciation for quantitative restrictions) leads to a surge of imports and to the export of capital via overinvoicing of imports because the public does not believe the policy will last. Put another way, expectations about success will influence the real interest rate that obtains during the transition, and that in turn will influence the prospects for success.

If expectations affect the smoothness of the transition to a sustainable equilibrium, or even the prospects of success in attaining a new equilibrium, how the program is presented and even who presents it become important. These two factors are not taken into account in the standard economic analysis of the content of stabilization programs. The relevant public must be persuaded that the program can work and that the government is determined to see that it will do so. How the rationale and content are presented will affect the way the public receives the program, as will the reputation of the public leaders responsible for seeing the program through. Programs identical in content might run smoothly in one setting and extremely roughly in another, and might even fail. The quality of political leadership, as well as the past experience of the public, is crucial in establishing favorable dynamics. A history of stability punctuated by one aberrant episode is likely to create a favorable environment for adjustment, with the public expecting a return to normalcy. If there is a history of instability and failed programs, the current program will be less likely to succeed because the public will be skeptical.[15]

Paradoxically, extreme instability, leading to hyperinflation, may improve the likelihood of success of a reasonably coherent program, because the public understands the extreme costs of continuing the preprogram situation, hopes the new program will succeed, and may be willing to give it a chance.[16] The public is willing to accept some austerity for the sake of fundamental and longer-run improvement. But even a favorable public reception cannot lead a technically flawed program to success. In particular, if budgetary and monetary conditions continue to be strongly expansionary, without adequate financing from abroad the stabilization program will unravel.

One useful function the International Monetary Fund can perform is to provide outside evaluation and sanction of a national program; that, plus a governmental commitment to the international community, through the IMF, to carry out the program, with disbursement of IMF or World Bank funds contingent on the attainment of certain policy targets, lends the program credibility. This credibility will be weakened if the IMF develops the reputation for agreeing to programs that have little chance of succeeding, as tended to occur during the late 1980s (see Sachs in Gwin and Feinberg et al. 1989).

Appendix

The relationship between expenditure, terms of trade, and output is shown in figure 2.1, which depicts the standard production possibility locus, QQ, for an economy that is small in the sense that it cannot influence its international terms of trade, defined as the price of its exports relative to the price of its imports. Initially our country is producing at the point Q_0, which indicates its production of nontradable goods (N) along the horizontal axis and its production of export goods (X) and consumption of imported goods (M) along the vertical axis. Its initial expenditure is at E_0, which is vertically above Q_0, indicating domestic absorption (public and private consumption plus investment) of the nontradables that are being produced and of import goods (M) measured along the vertical axis. The vertical difference $E_0 - Q_0$ is the trade deficit, which must be financed by the net inflow of foreign capital. Exports are represented by the height of Q_0.

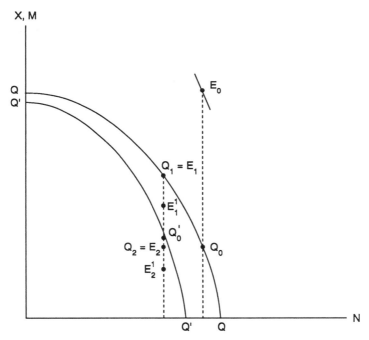

Figure 2.1
Production possibility: The relationship between expenditure, terms of trade, and output

Suppose now that the net flow of resources (net inflow of capital less debt-service payments) drops to zero, because foreigners, for whatever reason, no longer wish to invest in our country beyond their earnings on past investments. Then absorption must drop from E_0 to Q_0 because our country can no longer finance an import deficit. This will require a cutback of spending on imported goods (treated here as a composite of consumption and investment goods, which poses no problem as long as the prices of the import goods do not change relative to one another). But with such a cutback, Q_0 is not the best combination of imports and nontradable goods for our public to be consuming. There are too many nontradables relative to imports. We can change this mix by shifting resources out of N-goods into X-goods, along the production possibility frontier QQ, to a point such as Q_1, and exchange the additional export production for additional imports; this permits us to spend E_1 at Q_1 as long as the terms of trade have remained unchanged. Of course, at Q_1 the domestic price of nontradables has fallen relative to the price of tradables, a change that comes about because of the excess supply of N-goods at Q_0 and that is necessary to induce resources to shift from the production of N-goods to X-goods. The public is better off consuming at Q_1 than at Q_0, but is clearly worse off than it was at E_0.

If the international terms of trade have moved adversely for our country, a given volume of X-goods will buy fewer M-goods on the international market. In that event our consumption can no longer be at Q_1, but must drop to a point such as E_1^1, as a given level of exports will now buy fewer imports. (Of course, if the terms of trade improve, we could consume at a point vertically above Q_1.)

Reallocating resources from N-goods to X-goods cannot always be accomplished smoothly or costlessly. Labor and capital released from the now less profitable N-sector may not find immediate employment in the X-sector. How smoothly the reallocation occurs depends not only on the nature of technology in the X-sector relative to the N-sector, but also on the flexibility of factor prices and the mobility of factors of production. In the best of circumstances (easily movable factors, flexible factor prices), the country will shift resources smoothly along the QQ frontier from Q_0 to Q_1. In the worst of circumstances, where the output of N-goods has fallen and the output of X-goods has not risen, labor and capital will become idle in the N-sector and will not be absorbed into the X-sector, and output will be at Q_2. Without net resource inflows, consumption (plus investment) also must take place at Q_2, leaving the country worse off than it was even at Q_0. And if in addition the terms of trade have moved adversely, the country's absorption may have to drop further to a point such as $E\frac{1}{2}$.

Thus we can distinguish three sources of loss following a cessation of net resource inflows, all measured in terms of imports. The initial loss of imports is $E_0 - Q_0$, of which $E_1 - Q_2$ can be recouped provided labor and capital can be moved from N-goods to X-goods, leaving an unavoidable loss of the vertical distance between E_0 and E_1. If resources cannot be reallocated between sectors, there is the further loss $E_1 - E_2$, which, combined with the loss of imports, sums to the initial loss of resource transfers. In addition the output of nontradables has fallen by the horizontal distance between Q_0 and Q_2, a loss that is presumably temporary, although it may last for some time.[1] And if the terms of trade have worsened, there is the additional loss $E_2 - E\frac{1}{2}$.

At E_0 expenditure is divided between consumption (including government consumption) and investment. As noted above, investment is usually the first item to be cut in any macroeconomic retrenchment. This accomplishes the necessary reduction in current absorption, but it does so only by reducing the rate at which the QQ frontier is shifting outward, thus making possible greater output in future periods. Macroeconomic analysis is concerned with aligning E and Q on a sustainable basis (allowing for net resource flows) and moving along QQ as smoothly as possible in response to changing economic conditions, with as little loss of output as possible. A development or growth policy is concerned with the outward shift of the production possibility frontier. The two intersect insofar as imperfect macroeconomic policy slows the outward shift of QQ.

Two further points should be noted in figure 2.1. First, *any* movement along the production-possibility frontier from an initially optimal point such as Q_0 will lead to a recorded decline in the output of the economy when measured at the prices that prevailed at that point (indicated by the slope of the QQ frontier at that point). This will be true even when the country is better off at a different point on the production frontier owing to changed circumstances. Concretely, output at Q_1 is lower than output at Q_0 when measured at Q_0 prices, even though the country is better off at Q_1 than it would be at Q_0 in the absence of net resource inflows. In other words, the real GDP that is typically measured does not always adequately indicate the change in the well-being of a country due to unavoidably changed circumstances.[2]

Second, if our country has been importing capital from the rest of the world in the past, and if that capital has been used efficiently, it has shifted our production-possibility frontier outward, for example, from $Q'Q'$ in figure 2.1 to QQ. Provided the return to that investment exceeds the cost of servicing the debt, our country is better off than it would otherwise be even if the net resource inflow has turned *negative*, that is, even if debt-service obligations exceed new capital inflows. Reinterpreting the points in figure 2.1, our country is better off producing at Q_1 and consuming at E_1^1, the difference being debt-service payments, than it would be producing and consuming at Q_0' on $Q'Q'$, where no debt had been incurred. The difference $Q_1 - E_1^1$ is the return to foreigners on their past investment, leaving a net gain of $E_1^1 - Q_0'$, measured in imports, for our residents.

3   Generalizations and Lessons

A number of important lessons for developing countries emerge from the 1980s. Compared with the preceding thirty years, the 1980s cannot be considered a period of outstanding economic performance—for either these countries or the industrialized ones (see table 1.1).[1]

Economic Performance in the 1980s

After OPEC I, economic growth in the industrialized countries declined by nearly 2 percentage points, and this reduced rate continued throughout the 1980s. Growth rates would no doubt have declined over time as countries with low per capita output imported new technologies and moved closer to the technological frontier. But the sharp drop in the 1970s cannot be explained in that way, since it occurred in all the industrialized countries, including those (most notably the United States) that were at or near the technological frontier. Rather, it must be attributed to the dislocations created by the sharp increase in the price of oil—a critical input to most economic activity—combined with the policy reactions to this price increase and the uncertainties that ensued. Economic recession was the immediate consequence, with a sharp decline in investment; but another consequence was inflation, met at first by ambivalence, followed in the early 1980s by a strong anti-inflation stance in all the major developed countries.

Although inflation indeed dropped considerably from the nearly 10 percent a year reached in the period 1973–80, economic growth did not recover. Investment, especially in Europe, remained sluggish until the end of the decade and left growth flagging. Growth also fell in the developing countries after OPEC I, although the drop was concentrated in OPEC countries and reflected mainly a decline in the production of oil; non-oil-exporting countries actually increased their growth modestly. But whereas the growth of industrialized countries stabilized at the lower rate in the 1980s, in the developing countries it continued to fall. Their lead of a good 2 percentage points over the industrialized countries before 1980 shrank to about 1 percentage point in the 1980s, and that did not even compensate for the difference in population growth between the two groups. Moreover, it was mainly the industrialized countries that were able to put a lid on inflation; in many of the developing countries inflation merely spiraled ever higher.

As usual, the broad aggregates provide an overall picture but conceal enormous diversity. In both East and South Asia (dominated by China and India, respectively) economic growth was higher in the 1980s than it had been during the 1970s; and inflation was modestly lower. In contrast, economic growth dropped sharply in both Africa and the Western Hemisphere and inflation rose sharply in Latin America. Perhaps surprisingly, on average inflation remained roughly unchanged in Africa. A further decomposition of those regions would reveal similarly disparate developments in both growth and inflation. Although persistent high inflation is largely a Latin American phenomenon, several African countries—for example, Uganda and Zaire—seem to have fallen into the pattern, as well as Turkey.

Until the 1980s the countries of Central America plus Venezuela, on the other hand, could be reckoned among the countries with relatively low inflation, most of them having tied their currencies to the U.S. dollar (Panama actually used the dollar as its currency) and thus, roughly speaking, to inflation in the United States. Until then, high inflation had been prominent mainly in South America, but in the 1980s it spread to several Central American countries. During the period 1980–88 the average annual rate of inflation in the Latin American countries in our group never fell below 20 percent, whereas in the other countries, apart from Nigeria and Turkey, it never exceeded 13 percent, and in most cases was below 10 percent. Although outbursts of high inflation did occur in a number of countries—Korea and Sri Lanka in 1980, Nigeria in 1983–84, and the Philippines in 1984, for instance—the rate was quickly brought back below 20 percent, and often below 10 percent. Only in Latin America did it remain high year after year, although Mexico reduced its rate of inflation sharply at the end of the decade.

The rate of economic growth during the 1980s also varied greatly, ranging among our countries from a high of 8.4 percent a year in Korea to -0.4 percent a year in Argentina, with the Latin American countries all registering less than 4 percent and the Asian countries (including India) all registering more than 4 percent. Most of our countries experienced some decline in growth from the preceding decade, but surprisingly all the South Asian countries (plus Cameroon) showed some increase in growth in the 1980s compared with the period 1965–80. (See table 3.1, in which countries are ranked by their *trend* rate of growth over the period 1980–88.)

Reasons for Disparate Performance

What are the reasons for the sharp differences in economic performance among developing countries, even among oil-importing countries, all of which function in the same international economic environment? These differences are commonly attributed to four factors: the size of the external shocks to which countries were subjected, their historical experience with inflation, the extent to which their economies were outwardly oriented, and the degree to which their governments were authoritarian and thus presumably could control economic policy. As we shall shortly see, other reasons lie at the root of this disparity.

We have already touched on the size of the external shocks, whether measured in terms of the increased oil bill alone or total deterioration in the terms of trade (see tables 1.2 and 1.5). There is essentially no correlation between the size of the

Table 3.1
Average rates of growth and inflation (percent)

	Growth			Inflation		
	1960–73	1973–80	1980–88	1960–73	1973–80	1980–88
Korea 1967–88	8.2	8.5	9.3	11.2	17.5	8.7
Cameroon 1970–85	3.1	5.6	8.4	5.4	11.8	9.5
Pakistan	3.9	5.9	6.2	5.4	14.3	7.2
Thailand	8.0	7.4	5.9	3.1	11.8	5.9
India 1961–87	3.4	3.9	5.4	6.6	9.0	9.4
Turkey	5.7	4.5	5.4	6.0	38.6	50.1
Indonesia	5.2	7.9	4.7	75.7	20.8	10.0
Sri Lanka	3.6	4.6	4.3	3.3	10.0	13.0
Morocco	3.7	5.9	4.1	2.7	9.8	8.1
Kenya	5.7	5.8	3.9	2.8	13.9	10.9
Colombia	5.5	5.2	3.3	11.6	23.8	23.2
Brazil 1964–88	9.4	7.8	2.9	37.9	41.1	212.1
Costa Rica	6.4	5.2	2.4	3.4	13.0	28.3
Chile	3.6	2.5	1.9	66.2	206.7	21.8
Mexico 1965–86	7.1	6.7	0.4	3.9	19.7	74.5
Argentina	3.7	2.5	0.0	28.3	165.4	286.3
Nigeria	7.4	3.7	-0.1	5.3	16.7	17.8
Cote d'Ivoire 1976–83	NA	7.6	-1.2	3.9	15.5	6.4

Note: Countries are ranked by trend growth in GDP from 1980 to 1988; growth figures for 1960–80 are geometric averages from 1980 to 1988; inflation is measured by the consumer price index.
Source: Calculated from IMF, *International Financial Statistics*.

external shock in 1974 or in 1979–82 and economic performance during the 1980s.[2] Countries such as Korea and Sri Lanka had large negative shocks but rather good economic growth, whereas Nigeria and Mexico had positive shocks and poor growth. Although the size of the shock defined the size of the adjustment problem, it certainly did not determine the outcome in terms of economic growth. Some economies demonstrated much greater flexibility in adapting to external shocks than did others. Other things being equal, however, a negative shock is harmful. A substantial part of the deterioration in the economic performance of the Ivory Coast between the 1970s and the 1980s, for instance, was no doubt due to an exceptionally severe deterioration in its terms of trade around 1980. But that country made the mistake of treating a previous improvement in its terms of trade as a permanent one, thus greatly complicating its adjustment problem.

Inflation cannot explain the disparity in growth performance in the 1980s either. For our eighteen countries, there is a negative correlation between the rate of inflation and economic growth during this period, but it is not statistically significant. Nor did their prior history with inflation determine the rate of growth during the 1980s.[3] Brazil, for example, experienced high growth rates despite high inflation rates throughout the period 1965–80. India stands at the other extreme, with low inflation and low growth. But these countries are just the most striking examples. Although inflation undoubtedly distorts incentives and creates problems for those who must live with it, the proposition that inflation is a serious drag on growth does not stand up empirically.

Moreover, virtually all of our countries, including the rapidly growing Korea, experienced rates of inflation that were high by the standards of the industrialized countries during most of the 1970s and 1980s, even after allowing for the fact that rapid growth lends an upward drift to the consumer price index because the cost of labor services increases with wages.[4]

Sharp variations in inflation rates, however, can apparently retard growth. Because of the extreme turbulence they create, they discourage long-term investment and redirect entrepreneurial activity toward the exploitation of the economic rewards made possible by the turbulence. One reasonable measure of the variation in inflation had a negative correlation of .4 with the growth rate over the period 1980–88; moreover, a variation of 12.5 percentage point in inflation would reduce annual growth rates by 1 percentage point, a consequential amount. Among our countries, Argentina, Brazil, and Costa Rica all had variations in excess of 20 percent, and the figure for Mexico was almost as large (figure 3.1).[5] When we allow for other variables, however, this apparent effect becomes much smaller and statistically insignificant.

A third explanation frequently given for differences in growth performance and ability to absorb shocks is the external orientation of an economy, meaning that economic policy has concentrated on developing export markets rather than on import substitution. There is little doubt that over long periods of time an outward-looking policy facilitates economic growth, not least because it generates the physical capacity and marketing know-how needed to take advantage of selling possi-

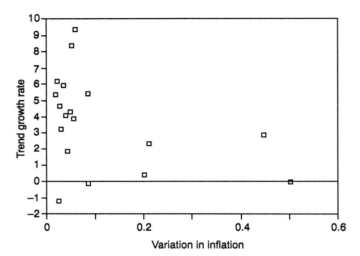

Figure 3.1
Growth and variation in inflation (eighteen countries, 1980–1988)

bilities worldwide and thus offers much greater scope for earning foreign exchange when that is especially necessary. Import substitution is by its nature limited by the size of the domestic market, product by product; for many products in many developing countries, the domestic market is quickly exhausted because of the limited purchasing power there. A spurt of growth therefore usually gives way to relative stagnation. Furthermore, import substitution tends to reduce the flexibility of an economy because the relatively easy substitutions are made, leaving the import bill made up of not easily substitutable essentials, such as foodstuffs, critical raw materials, or spare parts for foreign-made machinery.

Despite these well-known disadvantages of a policy of import substitution, the trade policy in each of our countries does not seem to have had an important influence on their ability to adjust to adverse external shocks. It is true that relatively open countries such as Korea and Thailand adapted rather well to the external shocks, and that relatively protectionist countries such as Argentina and Mexico had greater difficulty.[6] But some of the relatively open countries, such as Ivory Coast and Nigeria, also had a difficult time during the 1980s, whereas relatively protectionist countries such as India and Pakistan apparently dealt with the shocks with comparative ease.

It is difficult to measure trade distortions across countries. Although average tariff rates can be calculated, many developing countries rely heavily on import licensing, quantitative restrictions, and other nontariff distortions for limiting imports. In a recent comparative study, Michaely (1991) and his associates have attempted to measure the trend over time in import protection in nine of our eighteen countries. They caution against cross-country comparisons, but the authors attempted judgmentally to calibrate their measures of protection across their countries. Some results of this effort are reported in table 3.2, where the numbers represent points on a scale running from 0 (autarky) to 20 (free trade, apart from modest tariffs).

Four of the countries—Argentina, Brazil, Chile, and Colombia—had poor economic performance in the 1980s. The first two were relatively protectionist at the beginning of the decade, whereas the latter two were relatively open, although

Table 3.2
Trade liberalization index

	1974	1980	1985
Argentina	11	8	8[a]
Brazil	8	10	5
Chile	12	20	15
Colombia	12	14	8[b]
Indonesia	12	13	13[a]
Korea	14	16	18
Pakistan	10	9	9[b]
Sri Lanka	6	14	13
Turkey	5	6	15

a. 1982.
b. 1983.
Note: Index of degree of trade liberalization, with 20 representing effectively free trade. Numbers are not strictly comparable across countries, but have been calibrated by authors.
Source: Compiled from Michaely et al. 1991, pp.19–27.

both tightened import restrictions significantly in the early 1980s. Among the remaining five, all well-performing countries, three were relatively open, but Pakistan and Turkey were highly protectionist in 1980, although Turkey undertook a major trade liberalization in the early 1980s, as Chile and Sri Lanka had done in the late 1970s.[7]

Finally, it does not seem as though the form of government or the degree of political freedom had a significant bearing on the adaptability of our countries to external shocks and their subsequent performance. Four of our countries—Costa Rica,

Colombia, India, and Sri Lanka—were democracies (D) during the 1970s and early 1980s; three (Brazil, Indonesia, and Korea) were military or quasi-military autocracies (MA), although both Brazil and Korea later moved to elected governments; five (Cameroon, Ivory Coast, Kenya, Mexico, and Morocco) were civilian autocracies (CA), although Mexico's was notably different in character from the others; and six experienced changes in type of government (CG). Because Chile and Pakistan were military autocracies during most of the period, that leaves Argentina, Nigeria, Thailand, and Turkey as the countries that underwent significant change for our purposes. Broadly speaking, these last four can be considered politically unstable during the 1970s and early 1980s, along perhaps with the borderline cases of India (because of Indira Gandhi's national emergency in 1975) and Sri Lanka, (with its radical change in government and emerging civil war). The remaining countries were politically stable.[8]

The political dimension can be approached in a somewhat different way. The organization Freedom House has ranked countries since 1973 according to their degree of political rights and civil liberties (Gastil 1987). The greater the freedom, it might be thought, the greater the influence of special interest groups on economic policy making. Averaging Freedom House scores over the period 1973–85 produces a list that runs from Costa Rica, the most liberal, to Cameroon, the least. They can be somewhat arbitrarily divided into two groups, the more free and the less free, ranked from the highest to the lowest degree of freedom:

More free	Less free
Costa Rica (D)	Nigeria (CG)
Colombia (D)	Morocco (CA)
India (D)	Kenya (CA)
Sri Lanka (D)	Indonesia (MA)
Mexico (CA)	Pakistan (CG/MA)
Turkey (CG)	Korea (South) (MA)
Brazil (MA)	Chile (CG/MA)
Argentina (CG)	Ivory Coast (CA)
Thailand (CG)	Cameroon (CA)

The four most free countries are the democracies, and the least free ones are civilian autocracies, preceded by the military autocracies.

But is there any discernible relationship between the various political attributes of these countries—their form of government, political stability, or degree of political freedom—and economic performance? The issue can be formalized somewhat by dividing our countries into those that performed relatively well during the 1980s, following the shocks early in the decade, and those that performed relatively poorly. The main criterion will be economic growth (the upper half of table 3.1 shows the good performers), with some admixture of external debt problems and inflation. By these standards, the countries that performed badly during the 1980s are Argentina, Brazil, Chile, Colombia, Costa Rica, Ivory Coast, Mexico, and Nigeria; those that performed relatively well were Cameroon (which ran into some trouble only late in the decade), India, Indonesia, Korea, Morocco, Pakistan, Sri Lanka, and Thailand. In some respects, Turkey and Kenya are on the borderline, but because of Kenya's extraordinary growth in population it experienced a decline in per capita income, so should be grouped with the poor performers; Turkey, while a high inflation country, achieved a growth in per capita income in excess of 2.5 percent a year during the 1980s, so we include it among the good performers.

These classifications can be summarized as shown in table 3.3. Here we have called those with dramatic changes in government "unstable" and all others "stable," although, as noted

Table 3.3
Political stability and economic performance

Economic performance	Stable	Unstable
	Cameroon	
	India*	Thailand*
	Indonesia	Turkey*
Good	Korea	
	Morocco	
	Pakistan	
	Sri Lanka*	
	Brazil*	
	Chile	Argentina*
	Colombia*	Nigeria
Poor	Costa Rica*	
	Ivory Coast	
	Kenya	
	Mexico*	

*Countries in upper half of Freedom House list.

above, India and Sri Lanka might be considered borderline cases; Chile had a dramatic change to democracy in 1989, and both Brazil and Korea introduced elected governments less dramatically in 1985 and 1987, respectively.

It can be seen that no clear pattern emerges. An equal number of stable governments performed well and poorly, as was the case for unstable governments. Countries with a greater degree of freedom can be found in all four categories. Democracies and authoritarian governments alike can have poor— or good—economic performance. Simple generalizations about the effectiveness of different political systems in dealing with adverse—or favorable—external economic shocks do not seem to hold up. It is true that if we move India and Sri Lanka into the northeast, politically unstable, corner, then all the countries in the northwest corner (that is, those that are politically stable with good economic performance) will be civilian or military autocracies, all of which fall in the lower half of the Freedom House list. (Among these countries, however, Korea and Pakistan had free democratic elections in the late 1980s, and quite possibly Indonesia will follow in the 1990s.) Perhaps an authoritarian government has some edge when it comes to adopting difficult but desirable economic policies. Clearly, however, many authoritarian governments are not able or willing to do so, and the cases of India and Sri Lanka suggest that in some circumstances democratic governments in developing countries can also successfully implement policies of macroeconomic adjustment in response to adverse external shocks, which were admittedly modest relative to GDP in the case of India but were substantial for Sri Lanka.

If these explanations do not suffice, consider now some that do. Three factors seem to have played a vital role in the economic performance of the countries under consideration, beginning with the inflow of foreign resources. As we have seen, the extent of disabsorption required represents the immediate burden on any national economy and depends on many factors besides the direct external shock. Countries with an exceptionally poor performance were generally those that had to reduce their absorption by the greatest amounts and compress their imports; yet this was not closely correlated with the terms-of-trade and interest rate shocks of 1979–81. Put the other way around, countries that experienced sharp disabsorption between 1978 and 1983 also tended to perform poorly over the entire decade.

Second, economic performance was negatively influenced by the behavior of the real exchange rate. Policymakers can determine the nominal exchange rate of their currency relative to some leading currency, or basket of other currencies, and they can influence, if not always determine, the rate of inflation. Developments abroad are, of course, beyond their influence. The combination of inflation relative to that abroad, the choice of a nominal exchange rate, and the movements of leading currencies against one another together determine the real effective exchange rate, which in turn influences the competitiveness of a country's products on world markets. Steadiness in the real exchange rate has a strong influence on the stability of the economic environment in which business enterprises must make their investment and marketing decisions. A highly variable real exchange rate is likely to discourage efforts to develop new export markets.

Table 3.4 shows an index of the real effective exchange rate for our countries over the period 1978–88 (1980 = 100). The final column shows the coefficient of variation, a measure of the extent to which exchange rates moved during this period. Note that countries that performed relatively well during the 1980s also had relatively stable real exchange rates. There are, however, some notable exceptions. Brazil is known for its effective management of its exchange rate; its real exchange rate was relatively stable, despite high and highly variable rates of inflation. Similarly, Ivory Coast had a relatively stable real exchange rate, thanks largely to its membership in the West African Monetary Union. Yet the overall performance of both countries was rather poor during the 1980s (although Brazil had a surge in exports and in its merchandise trade surplus). Kenya, too, had a relatively stable real exchange rate, yet its economic performance, as argued above, was marginal. In contrast, both Indonesia and Turkey show a relatively high variation in their exchange rates, but their overall performance was not bad. In Turkey's case, however, the variation reflects a steady decline after 1979, presumably increasing the competitiveness of Turkish exports despite continuing inflation in that country.[9]

The third factor that seems to have played an important role is fiscal policy—or, more accurately, fiscal discipline—which in developing countries is closely related to monetary policy.

Table 3.4
Real effective exchange rates, 1978–1988

	1978	1979	1980	1981	1982	1983	1984	1985	1986	1987	1988	C.V. 78–88
Argentina	55	77	100	91	51	43	50	44	44	41	37	36
Brazil	123	113	100	121	128	104	104	100	95	95	103	10
Cameroon	103	102	100	92	90	93	95	99	110	123	119	10
Chile	85	86	100	118	107	87	85	69	58	54	51	26
Colombia	95	98	100	108	115	114	105	91	68	61	59	21
Costa Rica	87	91	100	64	73	83	82	81	73	66	60	15
Cote d'Ivoire	89	98	100	86	78	75	72	72	85	92	92	11
India	90	90	100	104	100	103	102	99	85	76	71	12
Indonesia	122	93	100	109	118	95	92	90	69	51	49	26
Kenya	104	101	100	97	100	95	102	100	87	79	73	10
Korea	98	107	100	104	107	103	101	96	81	80	89	9
Mexico	84	89	100	114	82	72	84	86	60	56	69	20
Morocco	103	103	100	92	90	84	79	74	71	69	67	15
Nigeria	91	94	100	111	114	134	185	166	91	29	30	44
Pakistan	102	100	100	113	104	100	102	95	79	70	97	12
Sri Lanka	81	87	100	106	113	112	125	117	104	93	91	13
Thailand	91	92	100	103	106	109	107	95	85	80	77	11
Turkey	118	128	100	98	84	81	78	78	65	62	62	24

Note: C.V. = coefficient of variation.
Source: IMF information notice system, real effective exchange rates corresponding to the quarterly report on exchange market developments.

Fiscal discipline is difficult to measure quantitatively across countries, but those who have observed a government in action can readily form a judgment on whether strong fiscal discipline is present. In particular, fiscal discipline is not well measured by the size of the budget deficit, because that can be large for a variety of reasons, some of which reflect no lack of fiscal discipline. A country that relies heavily on external financing in its major public infrastructure projects, for instance, might, during the peak period of construction, have a substantial budget deficit, but this might be accompanied by little monetary expansion or even (if the inputs are heavily imported) little pressure on the local economy. Fiscal discipline means that any deficit—whatever it may be—is run as a conscious matter with adequate financing and with the macroeconomic implications well thought out. Such discipline requires, among other things, control over the cash deficits of state-owned enterprises, so that their total borrowing can be integrated into macroeconomic management. Furthermore, spending by ministries must be subject to budget discipline—a point that seems obvious but in fact was violated in important ways in many of our countries at one time or another.

Sri Lanka, a country whose performance was relatively good during the 1980s, ran by far the largest deficit in 1980, whereas Chile, which performed less well, ran a substantial surplus (table 3.5).[10] Nearly half of the countries with deficits of 3 percent or more in 1980 were in the good performance list, and half of those with deficits of 3 percent or less performed relatively poorly. Clearly, budget deficits as such are not an

Table 3.5
Ratio of government surplus to GDP, selected years

Country	1972	1976	1980	1984	1988
Argentina	n.a.	-13.2	-3.5	-5.1	-2.6[a]
Brazil	-0.3	-0.2	-2.4	-4.8	-11.7[b]
Cameroon	n.a.	-2.3	0.5	1.6	-3.4[b]
Chile	-12.8	1.4	5.4	-3.0	0.0
Colombia	-2.5	1.0	-1.8	-4.3	-0.7[b]
Costa Rica	-4.3	-3.4	-7.4	-0.7	-4.5[a]
Cote d'Ivoire	n.a.	-1.0	-10.5	-3.1	n.a.
India	-4.3	-4.3	-6.5	-7.6	-7.7
Indonesia	-2.3	-1.4	-2.2	-0.6	-3.0
Kenya	-5.2	-5.4	-2.1	-3.1	-3.6
Korea	-3.8	-1.4	-2.2	-1.2	1.6
Mexico	-2.8	-4.4	-3.0	-7.1	-9.7
Morocco	-3.8	-17.6	-9.7	-6.0	-4.5[b]
Nigeria	0.3	-3.6	16.3	-4.1	-9.9[b]
Pakistan	-4.8	-9.3	-5.7	-6.2	-6.4
Sri Lanka	-7.7	-8.3	-18.3	-6.9	-12.6
Thailand	-4.2	-4.0	-4.9	-3.5	1.1
Turkey	-2.2	-2.0	-3.7	-10.0	-3.8

n.a. Not available.
a. 1986 figure.
b. 1987 figure.
Source: IMF, *International Financial Statistics* 80; World Bank data base.

important indicator of future performance. But all of the poor performers except Chile and, arguably, Colombia exhibited poor budgetary discipline during the early 1980s, in the sense that state-owned enterprises and sometimes spending ministries or provinces had direct access to foreign market funding (when available) and even to central bank funding, and total expenditures were far from being centrally controlled and monitored with macroeconomic considerations in mind. Budgeting virtually collapsed in Nigeria, and so far it has proved impossible to reconstruct spending totals even long after the spending occurred. All of the good performers, in contrast, kept total spending, with perhaps brief lapses, under tight central control and surveillance. Turkey moved from the former to the latter category in 1980. Six of the nine countries that showed an increase in the budget deficit between 1980 and 1984 were among the poor performers, whereas six of eight that showed a decline in the deficit were among the good performers. Again, this is not a perfect measure, but a suggestive one. Some countries, such as Mexico, reestablished tight budgetary control during the course of the 1980s, but only after much of the damage had been done.[11]

Stabilization and Growth

What can we say about the relationship between macro-economic stabilization and long-term growth? The answer, at least at a high level of generalization, is surprisingly little. For our collection of countries, considered as a cross section of developing countries, there is a weak negative relationship between growth in real output from 1965–88 and inflation over the same period. There is also a weak but not statistically significant negative relationship between growth and the annual variation in the terms of trade. However, no significant relationship is detected for either of these variables in 1980–88; nor is growth over the 1980s significantly related to the relative magnitude of the shock of the 1979–81 period, whether measured in the terms of trade or interest rate changes. However, growth over the 1980s *is* weakly but significantly (negatively) related to the annual variation in growth rates. In other words, stable growth seems to be conducive to higher growth. If a country can respond quickly and smoothly to internal and external disturbances, it is likely to be able to boost its overall growth rate.[12]

Why should this relationship hold? The answer lies in part in the fact that economic retrenchment, when it comes, falls disproportionately on public and private investment, thus reducing the future capital stock. This is especially true in programs that introduce large currency devaluations. Note that, in twenty-eight cases during the 1970s, investment in the two years following devaluation was cut an average of 13 percent. It is politically easier to reduce projects that have not yet started, or that have barely started, than to cut expenditures in progress.

Ironically, booms in public investment can also put a drag on long-term growth in developing countries, because they tend to be associated with ambitious politically motivated projects or with windfalls of revenue. In both cases, investment efficiency is usually low. At the same time, retrenchment may turn out to be helpful if projects of marginal (or negative) economic return are cut. But it is preferable to avoid both the booms and the subsequent retrenchment in the interests of long-term growth.

In developing countries, retrenchment following a balance-of-payments crisis has often included tighter restrictions on imports. Although such actions may be necessary in a real emergency, the restrictions tend to be difficult to remove once the crisis has passed, leaving a legacy of import restrictions that impede economic growth, as discussed extensively in the literature (see Little et al. 1970; Krueger 1978; Michaely et al. 1991). During the 1980s some reversal of this phenomenon became evident, as countries began to respond to external shocks by liberalizing imports (as Korea and Turkey did in 1981, and Mexico in 1987). In these cases, a severe crisis enabled governments to take actions that are likely to promote long-term growth but that might otherwise have been politically difficult.

What Lessons Can We Learn?

Some of the basic lessons that emerge from the experience of the eighteen countries considered here have to do with fiscal and exchange rate policy. These lessons are rather prosaic, but nonetheless important. On the fiscal (which in developing countries also implies monetary) front, *budgetary discipline* is the most important principle to observe at all levels of the economy, of the budget itself, and in all future obligations. Spending agencies must be under effective budgetary control and not have direct access to the central bank or the foreign capital market. What is not the same, *total* spending must also be under control to ensure that it falls within the government's capacity to finance it through revenues and borrowing that is not excessively inflationary. Even when non-inflationary sources of finance are available (for example, from abroad), discipline must be maintained over the total accumulation of debt, because debt-servicing obligations can greatly complicate future budgetary control and even bring an economy to the verge of a breakdown. As a result of heavy borrowing during the 1970s and 1980s, for instance, public interest payments in Mexico equaled two-thirds of total government revenues by 1988, and nominal interest payments in Argentina and Brazil exceeded total tax revenues. Such levels tightly constrain freedom of budgetary action.

The additional seigniorage made possible by inflation may be an efficient form of taxation, provided the rate of *inflation* remains moderate and reasonably steady. As the financial system evolves over time, the inflation tax base will erode, and new sources of revenue must be developed. But that process can take many years in a developing country. High inflation will more rapidly undermine the inflation tax. Accelerating inflation may temporarily restore it, but the gains are likely to be short-lived and may be offset by an erosion of the real value of other tax revenues. Furthermore, rapidly accelerating inflation badly distorts investment decisions and entrepreneurial activity, to the detriment of long-run growth. Accelerating

inflation is a symptom of underlying conflict over the dispo-
sition of national output, which must be resolved at the source,
that is, by achieving the minimal social consensus required to
cut particular expenditures or to raise particular taxes.

Large and erratic movements in the *real exchange rate*—defined
here in the operationally meaningful sense of a nominal exchange rate (or weighted average of rates) corrected for differential movements in factor costs—can be highly disturbing
both to a country's external accounts and to its domestic
economy. Large movements in rates clearly influence export
performance—in both directions. Substantial appreciation
discourages exports, as in Chile, Mexico, Nigeria, and a host
of other countries in the late 1970s and early 1980s; depreciation, in contrast, clearly encourages exports, as demonstrated
by Brazil, Chile, Mexico, Turkey, and others in the mid-1980s.
Depreciation is neither always necessary for good export
performance, as Thailand demonstrated in the 1980s, nor
sufficient, as shown by the poor export performance of Argentina despite substantial real depreciation (from a condition of
exceptional overvaluation) in the early 1980s. Other factors,
such as the structure of an economy's exports and the capacity
of its firms to respond to new export incentives, are also
important. Here is an area in which a flexible and adaptable
economy will perform better than one whose structure has
become rigid.

Movements in the real exchange rate may be necessary to
preserve or restore external equilibrium in the face of external
of internal disturbances. But in our eighteen countries the

large movements in rates were due mainly to policy-led developments in the domestic economy, although these were sometimes prompted or reinforced by external events.

If a country allows the exchange rate to appreciate inappropriately, it will eventually have to take the corrective step of devaluating its currency. Yet a large devaluation can be enormously disruptive to the domestic economy. First, by leading to a sharp increase in at least some prices, it risks triggering or reinforcing inflationary expectations, thus making more difficult the government's efforts to keep the economy on an even keel. In this connection, a once-off devaluation, keyed to a well-understood set of circumstances, is obviously less troublesome than a devaluation that is part of a pattern of seemingly desperate policy actions. Past experiences thus influence how public expectations will influence such relevant macroeconomic variables as the demand for money balances and investment. Moreover, for many countries a fixed exchange rate has been the main nominal anchor of the economy; if not properly handled, devaluation may undermine that role.

Second, a devaluation normally redistributes real income substantially, by virtue of the relative price changes it engenders, and that in itself is likely to induce economic contraction in the short run, because the losers—those whose incomes do not keep pace with the prices of the goods they consume—must cut their expenditures more rapidly than the rate at which gainers increase their expenditures. The redistribution may also open up political fissures by undoing a fragile social consensus on the prior distribution of income.

Third, currency devaluation affects the financial viability of all those entities—enterprises, financial institutions, or governments—that have financial obligations denominated in foreign currency without offsetting foreign income. With the growth of both public and private external debt during the 1970s and 1980s, currency devaluation came to have a far greater impact on debt-servicing capacity. Many countries introduced special exchange rates for the debt service following currency devaluation, sometimes lasting many years, to save indebted firms and agencies from bankruptcy, and in most cases the central bank defrayed the implicit subsidy. Sometimes the government or central bank simply assumed the external debt at the predevaluation exchange rate, becoming in turn a creditor of the enterprise in the domestic currency. These or similar arrangements were made in Brazil, Chile, Costa Rica, Mexico, and other countries (but not in Korea, which had been more prudent with respect to external borrowing and handled the special problems created by devaluation through low-interest loans made indirectly by the central bank, but without otherwise diminishing the external debt service).

These disadvantages of currency devaluation must be set against the occasional need to restore international competitiveness and shift resources from nontradable to tradable goods. This dilemma can be avoided by maintaining a relatively steady, or only slowly changing, real exchange rate. Steadiness in turn seems to be best attained with some variant of a crawling peg, or gliding parity, whereby a currency is fixed to a leading currency, such as the U.S. dollar, or to a basket of currencies relevant to the country in question, and the rate is changed by small amounts at frequent intervals. There is no pat formula by which the rate should change: correcting for differentials in GNP price deflators provides a useful starting point, to be altered by discretion if export competitiveness seems to be flagging or in response to shocks that require some change in the real exchange rate.

Countries should resist the temptation to fix the exchange rate *in order to* reduce domestic inflation, as Argentina and Chile did in the late 1970s. That will all but inevitably lead to real appreciation and a corrective currency devaluation, with its attendant costs. Retaining a fixed exchange rate when the underlying conditions have changed, as Costa Rica and Korea did in the late 1970s and Ivory Coast did throughout the 1980s, is also problematic. If the rate of domestic inflation has been brought in line with international levels through other means, however, allowing for differences in the stage of development, a country may wisely and successfully fix its exchange rate with respect to some leading currency or basket of currencies and thus reinforce stable price expectations.[13]

A third general policy lesson from the experience of the 1980s is that external shocks are extremely difficult to handle without some *external assistance*. The greatest deterioration in economic performance occurred in countries that were forced to convert payment deficits into surpluses quickly because the available financing was inadequate. In our collection of countries, this was true for Brazil, Ivory Coast, Kenya, and Mexico. If the external accounts must be improved quickly, practically the only way to do so is to compress imports. Particularly in countries that have previously encouraged heavy import substitution, that can be accomplished only by reducing investment and production. External resources, such as those provided by the IMF and the World Bank, permit a more gradual adjustment to the new situation. Needless to say, if a country relies on external financing in a period in which some retrenchment is required, it may be tempted to postpone the needed adjustment. This is what happened when countries resorted to extensive borrowing from commercial banks before the debt crisis of 1982 and even when some relied on official funding, as in the case of Ivory Coast before 1983. So appropriate actions should be a condition of external support. Where that combination exists, as in Korea and Turkey, difficult adjustments can be made with less loss of production and lower cuts in investment.

General Observations

Apart from these policy-specific lessons, some general observations can be made. All national economies are bound to have unexpected shocks. These may not be as big or as dramatic as the oil shocks of 1974 and 1979–80 but will nonetheless create a discernible disturbance. They may be demand shocks arising from booms and recessions in the industrialized countries, price shocks due to supply disturbances elsewhere in an integrated world market, or supply shocks related to strikes, earthquakes, or poor weather at home. Because such shocks can occur anywhere, it is all the more important for an economy to be flexible and adaptable and for policy makers to come forth with a timely and accurate analysis and response. To be able to absorb shocks with little discomfort is a desirable attribute.

Adaptability usually exacts a price, in that growth may be lower than would be possible under policies devoted to growth (or to any other single objective) in an environment of certainty, because the country must instead focus on hedging. For instance, it may have to maintain liquid international reserves against the contingency of an unexpected shortfall of export receipts or an unexpected need for imports, rather than convert them into fixed productive assets that can contribute directly and continuously to economic output. But in an uncertain environment adaptability will actually contribute to long-run economic growth, because inflexibility in the presence of shocks can be costly to growth.

A corollary of the usefulness of flexibility in the face of inevitable disturbances is that it is difficult to assess the relative contribution of external and internal factors in the response of a national economy to an economic disturbance. Whether or not disturbance is clearly external in origin, the response of the economy will depend heavily on internal factors—on its adaptability, hence on the cumulative impact of past developments, including past policies—and its subsequent performance will bear no relationship to the size of the initial adverse impact, as we saw in the case of the oil shocks of 1974 or 1979–80. External events may precipitate a disturbance, but it usually takes internal factors to convert the disturbance into a crisis. This departs from the view that developing countries are by and large blameless and perform poorly because of an adverse external environment, or the view that all economic problems in developing countries are due to their own poor or inadequate policies. More often than not, reality is a complex mixture of the two.

The condition of an economy when an exogenous shock hits, whether it is internal or external in origin, strongly influences its ability to deal with the shock. Moreover, since this condition is the cumulative result of past events and policies, history is important. An economy's historical experience—including the memories and interpretation of that experience by both policy makers and the general public—can either narrow or enlarge the policy options available for responding to a new disturbance. This condition is also a product of public perception of the competence and determination of the government to carry out its announced actions—in short, the credibility of the policy. A government with high credibility has greater scope for influencing events, because the public is more likely to believe what it says and to respond accordingly. Admittedly, credibility can be dissipated with inept pronouncements and actions.

Beyond this historical point, current domestic circumstances may also determine how easily the country adjusts to an exogenous shock. If for domestic reasons the country responds by undertaking contractionary actions, the disturbance, although aggravating the situation, may reinforce the public's perception of the need for contraction and thus evoke public cooperation. This situation seems to have occurred in both Korea and Turkey in the late 1970s. If, in contrast, the country has recently launched an ambitious expansionist program when the disturbance occurs, as in the Ivory Coast in the late 1970s, then it will be more difficult to muster support for turning the policy around to deal with the disturbance.

Since there is unlikely to be any correlation between the evolution of domestic economic policy in individual developing countries and the exogenous shocks they experience, how well they adjust to these disturbances depends in part on *luck*.

Positive shocks—those that raise the national income of a country—are often a mixed blessing. Countries that fail to handle such shocks skillfully are likely to experience later difficulties, especially if the shock is temporary. They can expect two kinds of difficulties.

The first concerns government behavior in response to public expectations. Apparently governments are unable to receive additional revenue without feeling under irresistible pressure to spend it. If receipts go up, government spending all but invariably increases. Sometimes, as in the case of Mexico and Nigeria in the early 1980s, it exceeds the actual increase in receipts, in anticipation of future receipts. Notable exceptions to this pattern are Cameroon and (outside our sample of countries) Kuwait, both of which succeeded in sequestering a substantial portion of their increased oil revenues following the 1979–80 increase in oil prices. Governments typically behave as if positive shocks are permanent and negative shocks are temporary. With higher revenues, they are likely to increase not merely government investment but also ongoing government programs and public employment, both of which are difficult to reverse when revenues decline.

The second difficulty has to do with the response of an economy to a boom in exports of its primary products. In adjusting to a new equilibrium, countries tend to depress the production of other tradable goods—often foodstuffs and sometimes manufactures—and stimulate the production of nontradable goods and services. Such adjustments may be optimal (that is, income maximizing) if the export boom is permanent. But the adjustment usually starts in response to a boom that is neither clearly temporary nor permanent. Such adjustments are often difficult to reverse once tilled land has been abandoned, for example, and manufacturing firms have gone bankrupt. Booms are not easy to handle, unless the government is the initial recipient of the increased income (as is the case in most oil-exporting countries). And even there, as we have seen, governments find it difficult to sequester the increased income.

Perhaps the most notable feature of the experiences of these eighteen countries is their rich diversity. Examples can be found of many theoretically ambiguous possibilities, and for every simple substantive generalization there is almost always an exception. This finding implies that behavioral relationships (as distinguished from balance sheet and income expenditure identities, which always hold) should be analyzed in the framework of the actual situation prevailing in each country. Although generalizations can be made about the behavior of governments and of private agents in crisis situations, these generalizations are rarely universal and should always be tested against the experience and circumstances of each particular country.

4   The Lingering Problem of Developing-Country Debt: Origins

It has been nearly a decade since the Mexican debt crisis burst upon the scene. Commentary at that time gave the impression either that the problem would certainly have been "solved" by as distant a date as 1990, or that major default would have occurred, creating deep and possibly unmanageable fissures in the world financial system. Reality is typically more prosaic. The debt problem has not been "solved" in the sense that many countries are still heavily burdened not only by debt but also by their current servicing obligations, reschedulings are now commonplace, and arrearages continue to be large and widespread. On the other hand, the banking system has not collapsed, and major threats to it, particularly in the United States, come from sources other than developing-country debt. In the meantime, many debt-ridden countries experience poor economic performance, entailing both economic and social hardship, as they struggle to deal with their external financial obligations.

This chapter will first characterize briefly the situation in the late 1980s and then analyze, perhaps unconventionally, how

we got into the debt mess. The next chapter addresses a
number of solutions that have been proposed to deal with the
situation, concluding that there is no superior alternative to
continuing ad hoc management, but suggesting that management should be tilted more toward economic revival and less
toward rigorous compliance with contractual financial obligations.

A Brief Status Report

By the end of 1986, total external debt, short-term as well as
long-term, of developing countries exceeded one trillion U.S.
dollars, well over twice what it had been at the end of 1978
(table 4.1).[1] In relation to gross domestic product (GDP, the
total output of each country), external debt had increased from
26 to 38 percent over the same period, and debt servicing
(interest and amortization payments on long-term debt) had
reached 22 percent of export earnings, up from 19 percent in
1978.

These global figures of course obscure a wide diversity of
experience among developing countries. Table 4.1 shows separately the two regions with the most serious debt problems,
Latin America and Sub-Saharan Africa. African debt nearly
doubled in relation to GDP over the period 1978 to 1986 and
was nearly twice as high as the average for all developing
countries. Because most of the lending was governmental, and
much of it was on concessional terms, debt-servicing payments—at 21 percent of exports—were only slightly higher

Table 4.1
External debt and debt service

	1978	1980	1982	1984	1985	1986	1987	1988	1989	1990e
Developing countries										
External debt ($bn)	399	636	836	926	998	1095	1212	1216	1214	1265
Debt/GDP (%)	26	24	31	34	36	38	38	35	32	30
Debt/exports (%)	132	82	120	134	151	172	161	142	128	124
Debt-servicing ratio (%)	19	13	19	20	21	22	19	19	16	16
Western hemisphere										
External debt ($bn)	156	231	331	359	369	384	416	401	399	408
Debt/GDP (%)	32	35	44	46	45	44	44	39	37	35
Debt/exports (%)	217	184	271	275	296	350	345	292	272	264
Debt-servicing ratio (%)	38	33	53	42	41	45	36	45	35	35
Sub-Saharan Africa[a]										
External debt ($bn)	30	44	54	58	67	78	92	95	98	107
Debt/GDP (%)	36	39	51	57	63	64	71	66	68	69
Debt/exports (%)	141	148	214	221	262	294	320	323	320	345
Debt-servicing ratio (%)	15	17	22	24	22	21	18	20	22	24

Notes: External debt excludes debt owed and debt service paid to the IMF. All ratios are end-of-year debt as percentage of the year indicated. Debt-service payments are actual payments of interest on total debt plus actual amortization payments on long-term debt.
a. Excludes Nigeria and South Africa.
e = Estimated.
Source: IMF, *World Economic Outlook*, May 1990, tables A45, A48, and A49.

than average. In contrast, Latin America—where most of the debt was owed to commercial banks at commercial interest rates—paid out nearly 45 percent of its export earnings to service its external debt.

Even these regional totals conceal wide variation among countries. For instance, Chile and Costa Rica had a debt-to-GDP ratio of over 60 percent, and Somalia had a debt-to-GDP ratio in excess of 100 percent, with scheduled debt-service payments equal to 97 percent of projected exports in 1986–87; Sudan had scheduled payments of 150 percent of projected exports (World Bank 1986, table A.4). Needless to say, these latter two countries did not pay all the interest due. In 1985 thirty-one debt reschedulings took place, nineteen with government creditors and twelve with commercial banks, covering $93 billion in debt. Agreements on another $26 billion were pending at year end (United Nations 1986, p.80). Although the peak was reached in the mid-1980s in terms of both number of countries and amounts of debt covered, seven countries rescheduled a total of $52 billion in debt in 1989.[2] These reschedulings represent both a symptom of and a response to the debt problem.

In other words, some countries were not in fact meeting their scheduled obligations, and others did so only by having rescheduled their obligations. Moreover, the extensive servicing that took place was made possible in some cases only by a severe compression of imports, which both resulted from and contributed to a marked slowdown in domestic economic growth compared with that of the 1960s and 1970s. For instance, gross investment relative to GDP fell by about 8 percentage points in the four largest Latin American countries between 1976–81 and 1984 (United Nations 1986, p.116). Real per capita GDP was about 10 percent lower in Africa and Latin America than it had been in 1980 (United Nations 1986, p.28), and real per capita income was lower still by 1–2 percentage points because of an adverse movement in their terms of trade. Again, there was substantial variation in the performance of individual countries. To be sure, the worst seemed to be over for most countries in this respect, as positive economic growth resumed after the declines of 1982–83. But in many countries there was still a legacy of high urban unemployment and much lower investment than had been typical before the emergence of the debt crisis.

Overall, however, 1986 seems to have been the nadir. Thereafter, thanks partly to the recovery of oil prices in 1987, the debt/export ratio declined for all developing countries taken as a group, and for the western hemisphere. Sub-Saharan Africa, unfortunately, did not participate in this general improvement; there the debt situation continued to worsen.

The creditor banks—at least in the United States, for which more comprehensive figures are available—managed to reduce their relative exposure to developing countries, as loans to such countries fell from 10.3 percent of total assets in 1981 to 8.2 percent in 1985, and the same loans dropped from 192 percent of total capital in 1981 to 118 percent in 1985, the last figure being well below the 144 percent it was in 1978 (UNCTAD 1986, pp.68, 169). By the end of 1989 both ratios had dropped further, to 4 percent and 48 percent, respectively.

The outlook for the 1990s of course depends on many variables, among them growth and inflation rates in the OECD countries, policies of adjustment in the indebted countries, interest rates, oil prices, exchange rates, and so on. It is impossible to predict with confidence what will happen. One plausible scenario has been developed by the UNCTAD staff. This scenario assumes that the OECD countries grow at 3 percent per annum over the period 1990 to 2000, and the developing countries grow between 4.5 and 5 percent. Short-term interest rates on dollar assets are assumed to be 8 percent. The main implications for debt are shown in table 4.2. Overall debt and interest payments decline relative to exports over the decade after 1990 by substantial amounts, suggesting a gradual dissipation of the debt problem.

Again, however, there is a substantial dispersion among countries. Thanks largely to export growth, the improvement for Latin America as a whole is dramatic (with the debt/export ratio declining over 50 percent); but Africa experiences much less improvement, especially in interest payments as a share of projected exports.

There is no magic in any particular debt/export ratio or debt-servicing ratio. If a country can invest profitably at rates well in excess of its borrowing costs (where profitability is measured in terms of foreign currency), it could in principle sustain quite high debt/export ratios and still leave the country in a superior position to what it would experience with lower debt. Cooper and Sachs (1985, pp. 45–46), for instance, offer a numerical example with plausible assumptions that yields a debt/GNP ratio of 2, considerably higher than any

Table 4.2
Medium-term debt scenario, 1988–2000

	1988	1990	1995	2000
All developing countries				
Debt/exports (%)	136.6	118.7	82.2	59.9
Interest payments/exports (%)	8.9	8.0	5.3	3.6
Latin America				
Debt/exports (%)	299	261.8	170	105.2
Interest payments/exports (%)	23.3	21.5	14.1	8.8
Africa				
Debt/exports (%)	389.2	394.1	320.1	282.9
Interest payments/exports (%)	18.6	21.4	17.9	15.1

Notes: Latin America includes the Caribbean.
Source: UNCTAD, *Trade and Development Report 1989*, table 15, p. 29.

that we actually observe, and a debt-servicing ratio of 50 percent, yet lowering these debt ratios would worsen the country's welfare. But this kind of example assumes both efficiency in domestic investment and a ready market for the products of the debtor country—two conditions that have not always been met in recent years.

How Did We Get into the Debt Crisis?

The 1980s were difficult for creditors and debtors alike, and the debt situation has even been thought to threaten the functioning of the entire world economy. It is natural to ask how we got into this mess. Two views are especially popular. One places responsibility overwhelmingly on the commercial banks. A typical expression of this view, appearing in commentary on the Bradley proposal, is as follows: "Best of all, the Bradley proposal would finally make commercial banks pay their share of the cost of managing the debt crisis. Back in the 1970s, the banks were only too happy to lend Latin America all the money it wanted, but they have so far managed to stick others with the losses they deserve for their failing. It's way past time for the banks to pay their share." (*New Republic*, July 28, 1986, p. 9). On this view, if only the banks had not engaged in folly in pursuit of greed, the debt crisis would not have arisen.

An alternative view points to the debtor countries: if only they had not engaged in grandiose and ill-conceived investment projects of doubtful economic value, or in consumption binges, or if they were not corrupt, or if they did not countenance massive capital flight by their citizens, including government officials, debt might have been a problem, but it would not have created a crisis.

I believe that both of these views, while indulging a natural human penchant for finding a scapegoat, are fundamentally misleading. In contrast, it is arguable that all institutions were performing their functions more or less appropriately, given the circumstances in which they found themselves. This is not to say that there were no mistakes. There were many mistakes, both by borrowers and by lenders. Some so-called investment projects were dubious from the outset, and some loan officers were no doubt both aggressive in their pursuit of borrowers and careless in their analysis of the borrowers' prospects. But there are always such mistakes. They are being made even now. Mistakes do not typically create global crisis. The international financial system is resilient enough to accommodate many mistakes, and to work out of them.

What then went wrong? It is useful to recall a bit of history covered in chapter 1. The first major oil price increase occurred in 1974 and produced surpluses of over $60 billion in the members of OPEC. The second large oil price increase occurred in 1979–80, and produced surpluses in excess of $100 billion in OPEC, in each case with corresponding deficits in the oil-importing countries. The major countries contracted economically on both occasions, and that contraction actually worsened the situation of many developing countries, who depend crucially for their export earnings on buoyant markets in the industrialized world.

Because of the low short-run price elasticity of demand for oil, adjusting at once to the two major oil price shocks would have required a world depression to reduce the quantity of oil needed by oil-importing countries enough to eliminate the large OPEC surpluses. Depression as a by-product of instantaneous adjustment could have been avoided only if one thinks the oil price would have cracked quickly under the pressure of a decline in demand. It did not respond significantly to declining demand in 1975. It did finally crack in late 1985, but that was three years after the recession of 1982. It took eleven years and two major world recessions after the first oil price increase to realize the 1974 forecast by some eminent economists that OPEC would "collapse," like all previous cartels had done. In short, "recycling" the OPEC balance-of-payments surpluses in retrospect still seems to have been a desirable way of handling a regretable problem. But the inevitable consequence of such recycling was a growth of external debt, which was cumulatively substantial.

Even after allowing for such recycling to oil-importing countries, however, it remains something of a puzzle why bankers continued to lend heavily to Mexico (and to Bolivia) in 1981 and early 1982, when it was clear to those who looked closely that the Mexican government was in the spending phase of its presidential cycle, while maintaining a fixed exchange rate during a period of accelerating inflation—normally an unsustainable combination. But it is necessary to recall the frame of mind that was widespread at the time with respect to future prospects of oil and gas. Some U.S. buyers had paid over nine dollars per thousand cubic feet for gas at the wellhead in 1981 (compared with an average price in the late 1980s of around two dollars), and oil, at thirty-five dollars a barrel, was thought to be on a rising slope to at least fifty dollars a barrel within the foreseeable future. With their large oil and gas reserves, countries such as Bolivia, Mexico, Nigeria, and Venezuela were thought to have ample collateral. This view was shared by both borrowers and lenders; no one was fooling anyone; there were no asymmetries of information. Everyone simply proved to be wrong in valuing this collateral, at least within the relevant time horizon. They were wrong in part because their analysis was wrong; they extrapolated short-run price inelasticity of demand for oil into the longer run, without allowing both for new supplies and for extensive conservation even at the thirty-five dollar price, certainly in the prospect of fifty dollars a barrel. But they were also wrong in part because their implicit forecast of official behavior was fundamentally wrong. A major violation of expectations was shared by both borrowers and lenders.

If we leave aside the special case of Poland, the debt crisis erupted as a global crisis starting with Mexico in August 1982. That year was characterized by a deep recession, from which in some respects the world did not recover until 1988. But the important point is that it was an *unexpected* recession. The Reagan administration had forecast 3 percent growth during the course of the year (from the fourth quarter of 1981 to the fourth quarter of 1982), on the dual supposition that in the proper expectational environment money supply only influences prices, not real magnitudes, and that the 1981 tax cut would release the tax-inhibited latent energies of the American people in the pursuit of economic growth.

One could plausibly discount the forecasts of an administration exuberantly enthusiastic about its own theories and programs, and to some extent the "market" did discount it. The Federal Reserve had a more somber view of the outlook. Members of the Federal Open Market Committee (FOMC, in charge of framing monetary policy) projected growth of 0.3 to 3.0 percent during 1982, with inflation (measured by the GNP deflator) expected to run around 7 percent, and with unemployment by the fourth quarter of 1982 expected to be in the range of 8.25–9.5 percent, up somewhat during the course of the year. In view of these expectations, they established in early 1982 a target range for growth in money supply (M1) of 2.5–5.5 percent (Federal Reserve Board, *Monetary Policy Objectives for 1982*, Feb. 10, 1982).

Private forecasters also had a more somber view. In early 1982, after the recession (as we now know) had already started, Data Resources, Inc. forecast a 2 percent growth between the fourth quarter of 1981 and the fourth quarter of 1982. One of the nice features of DRI forecasts is that they give some notion of the confidence the forecasters hold in it. At that time DRI actually allowed that there was a possibility of a recession during 1982, with an expected decline of 1.1 percent in real GNP, with the upturn to begin in the third quarter of 1982. They attached a probability of only 15 percent to this recession forecast.

In the end, real U.S. GNP actually declined over the four quarters to the end of 1982 by 1.5 percent, and unemployment climbed to 10.6 percent. Nominal GNP during the year grew by only 2.6 percent, far below the 8–10.5 percent expected by the FOMC members. Both prices and real output grew dramatically less than expected.[3]

Normally the impact of a recession, which weakens markets for the exports from developing countries, is mitigated by a decline in interest rates, thus relieving some of the pressure on debtors. But during the first half of 1982 nominal interest rates on U.S. Treasury bills averaged 12.6 percent, even while output was falling. They declined in the second half of the year, partly in response to the emerging debt crisis, but at 8 percent remained very high for a depression year. Moreover, interest rate spreads widened on lower-quality assets, so that many interest rates did not experience the full decline in Treasury bill rates. Libor, for instance, averaged 13.3 percent during 1982, compared with 10.7 percent for Treasury bills, whereas normally the spread is only about 1 percentage point. And spreads over Libor on bank lending also widened.

The U.S. recession was reinforced by contractionary fiscal action and tight monetary policy in Japan, Germany, Britain, and several other countries. The dollar rose sharply in value during this period, aggravating further the problem for countries with debt denominated in dollars but with export sales denominated in other currencies.

An unexpectedly sharp and prolonged economic contraction always works hardship on debtors and, through their defaults, on creditors. Both find that calculations of investment returns that were perfectly valid when made are suddenly invalidated by the new economic environment. Some borrowers have enough financial cushion to carry themselves through the slump until better times ahead; others do not, develop arrearages, and even go into bankruptcy. In a domestic context, bankruptcy leads to foreclosure, financial reorganization, or liquidation with partial payment to creditors. Of course, some investments may have been ill-conceived even in better economic conditions. But the point to emphasize is that many basically sound investments, even with the allowance for a margin of error, can turn sour if the conditions on which they were predicated worsen sharply and unexpectedly.

On this view of the matter, it could be said that the Federal
Reserve and its administration supporters were directly responsible for the debt crisis, for it was the Fed that tightened
money so sharply in 1980 to 1982. On the other hand, the Fed
was just doing the job it was expected to do. In 1980 there was
a universal clamor, by governments of developing countries
as well as those of industrialized countries, for a reduction in
world inflation. Everyone wanted lower inflation, but few
reckoned on the costs. The Fed proceeded in the only way it
knew how, by tightening money and raising short-term interest rates. It briefly embraced monetarism, so it could persua-
sively allow "the market" to determine interest rates and shun
direct responsibility for their levels. But it pursued monetary
targets such that a sharp rise in interest rates was predictable.
What was not predicted, as the above forecasts suggest, was
that the U.S. economy would respond so sharply to the tightened monetary conditions as to raise unemployment nearly to
11 percent. So the Fed evidently over-tightened monetary
policy in terms of its own expectations. But the result—brought
on in part by the sharp appreciation of the dollar, which had
not been factored adequately into the calculation—was a
dramatic drop in the rate of U.S. and subsequently world
inflation, an objective that was universally proclaimed.

Given that world disinflation could not be achieved costlessly,
it can still be asked why the developing countries had to bear
a disproportionate share of the cost. But did they? Those who
put the question often forget that the industrial world also
went through a great wrenching after 1981. Unemployment
reached nearly 11 percent of the civilian labor force in the

United States, and while that gradually receded after early 1983, unemployment in Europe continued to grow into the mid-1980s, exceeding 13 percent in Britain and 20 percent in Spain. Investment in the industrialized countries, as in Latin America, was severely depressed, presaging a lower income for many years to come.

Altogether, the United States probably lost nearly $700 billion in output (measured in 1982 dollars) over the period 1981–84 due to the increase in unemployment and the emergence of excess productive capacity; the loss in other OECD countries would double that staggering loss. Both firms and workers suffered.

Although the U.S. economy recovered, it did so in a lopsided way because of the continuing strength of the dollar, so that firms and farms that sell tradable goods felt exceptionally stiff competition from foreign goods, whose manifestation was a U.S. trade deficit in excess of $100 billion a year from 1984 through 1989. The rate of business failures in the United States in 1983 was over four times what it had been in the late 1970s, and nearly twice the rate in the previous recessions of 1970 and 1975. The banks of the industrialized countries experienced a sharp loss of earnings and a depression of stock values. Sachs and Huizinga (1987, p.581) estimated that in 1983 stock prices of the leading U.S. banks were depressed by 15 cents for each dollar of Latin American debt in their portfolios; by 1986 that figure had risen to 46 cents. Over the 1980s nearly 1,000 U.S. banks closed due to bad claims on domestic borrowers caught in the same violation of expectations as foreign borrowers were.

So, developing countries were not the only parties to suffer, but they suffered extensively. The broad macroeconomic variables are shown in table 4.3. The OECD recession of 1982 reduced developing-country growth in 1982–83, and after 1984 it remained roughly 1 percentage point below what it had been in the 1970s. The terms of trade of all developing countries worsened after 1980 and remained weak throughout the 1980s, whereas real interest rates were substantially higher than they were in the 1970s.

Table 4.3
Economic growth, inflation, interest rates, and terms of trade (percent per annum)

	1972–81	1982	1983	1984	1985	1986	1987	1988	1989	1990ᵉ
OECD growth	3.0	-0.4	2.6	4.8	3.4	2.7	3.5	4.4	3.4	2.6
OECD GDP price deflator	8.8	7.2	5.3	4.6	3.7	3.4	2.9	3.2	3.9	3.9
LDC growth	5.0	0.6	1.9	3.8	3.9	4.0	3.8	4.1	3.0	2.2
LDC terms of trade	-0.8	-1.5	-1.0	2.5	-0.1	0.0	-0.9	1.7	-0.1	-3.3
Libor	9.6	13.6	9.9	11.3	8.6	6.8	7.3	8.1	9.3	8.3
Libor minus OECD deflator	0.8	6.0	4.4	6.4	4.9	3.4	4.4	4.9	5.4	4.4

Notes: Real GDP averages for country groups are weighted by the average U.S. dollar value of their respective GDPs (GNPs where applicable). Average 1972-81 is compound annual rates of change. OECD inflation averages weighted by the average U.S. dollar value of their respective GNPs over the preceding three years. London interbank offer rate on six month U.S. dollar deposits. LDC terms of trade is for non-fuel exporter developing countries. e = Estimated.
Source: IMF, *World Economic Outlook*, October 1990, tables A1, A5, A8, a28; IMF, *International Financial Statistics*.

Moreover, after 1981 the net flow of capital into developing countries dropped sharply, in response to the debt crisis and doubts about the ability of developing countries to service their debts. As the consequence, therefore, of (1) stagnant export earnings, (2) a worsened terms of trade, (3) a rise in interest payments, and (4) a decline in capital inflows, the capacity to import of developing countries was sharply reduced (recall table 2.1), and this in turn required cuts in both public and private consumption and especially in investment. This is not to say that poor economic performance was due solely or even mainly to external debt. As we saw in chapter 3, domestic policies interact with external developments to determine the circumstances of each country, and economic policies were poor in many debt-ridden countries.

Table 4.4 shows export earnings, net interest payments, and the net transfer of resources into all capital-importing developing countries. The net transfer of resources in current dollars worsened by $63 billion between 1980 and 1985, nearly half of which was due to higher interest payments and the remainder to a decline in net capital inflows of all kinds (including direct investment net of foreign earnings on direct investment). By 1985 Latin America was transferring $30 billion to the rest of the world, whereas the net transfer into Sub-Saharan Africa was below half earlier levels. It is this decline in the transfer of resources, not compensated by commensurate increases in exports, that has put the financial squeeze on developing countries.

The drop in capital flows, almost all of which was in commercial bank lending, was the result of financial institutions doing

Table 4.4
Factors affecting capacity to import by capital-importing developing
countries ($bn)

	1980	1982	1984	1985	1986	1987
Merchandise exports	388.2	379.7	404.7	391.8	373.2	437.5
Net interest paid	-24.7	-51.2	-53.2	-52.8	-49.8	-49.0
Net transfer of resources	40.3	11.8	-9.5	-22.7	-20.1	-22.5
Net transfer of resources by region						
Highly indebted middle income[a]	21	-10	-23	-32	-20	-18
Sub-Saharan Africa[b]	9.8	8.4	3.3	4.1	6.1	7.2

Notes: Net transfer of resources is net capital flow minus the net payment
of interest and dividends; it includes direct investment, private credit flows,
and official flows.
a. The middle-income group comprises Argentina, Bolivia, Brazil, Chile,
Colombia, Cote d'Ivoire, Ecuador, Mexico, Morocco, Nigeria, Peru, the
Philippines, Uruguay, Venezuela, and Yugoslavia.
b. Sub-Saharan Africa excludes Nigeria and South Africa.
Source: United Nations, *World Economic Survey 1988*, pp.50–51.

what they though best, under the new circumstances. Lending
did not look nearly so attractive in the economic conditions of
post-1982, in part because of the global economic recession, in
part because loans by any one bank might be put in jeopardy
by withdrawals by other banks. As noted in chapter 2, this
latter effect is perfectly rational from the perspective of an
individual lender, but not from a global perspective. It results
in a liquidity crisis.

To sum up, then, contrary to widespread assumption, there
are no villains in the piece. Rather, there are many parties
doing their jobs more or less appropriately, adapting as overall

circumstances change, with the usual number of mistakes—
all of which added up, as can always happen following a stark
change in policy, to a global crisis. (If villains must be found,
they are the Shah of Iran, who pushed through the first major
oil price increase in December of 1973, and the Ayatollah
Khomeini, who led the Iranian revolution in 1979. But each of
them was doing what he thought best for his country, as rulers
or would-be rulers should.)

The sharp drop in oil prices in late 1985 and early 1986, from
$27 to under $15 a barrel, imposed a new shock on the world
economy, once again redistributing adjustment burdens
sharply. It eased the debt problems of most indebted developing countries, but considerably worsened the debt problems of Ecuador, Indonesia, Mexico, Nigeria, Venezuela, and
several other net oil- or gas-exporting debtor nations. Even
with the relief of lower nominal interest rates and lower oil
prices, many oil-importing nations still had serious debt-
servicing problems—not least because the drop in oil price
was itself associated with a slackening of economic growth in
the industrialized nations and with a decline of many commodity prices other than oil.

Historical and Domestic Solutions

Debt problems, even global debt problems, are not new. There
were extensive defaults on external debts during the Great
Depression of the 1930s, and of course arrears and default are
a frequent occurrence in any rapidly changing economy, with

ups and downs in aggregate demand and shifts in the pattern
of demand and output. It is instructive to explore briefly how
these debt problems have been dealt with.

A comprehensive history has yet to be written on the defaults
of the 1930s. Recent experience has revived interest in the
period, and better information and analysis are becoming
available.[4] Many debtors, both private and governmental,
went into default on interest and amortization payments
during the 1930s. The defaults were concentrated in Eastern
Europe (including Germany) and Latin America. Some hard-
pressed debtors, such as Argentina and Uruguay, did not
default, in these cases under severe pressure from their British
creditors. Publicly issued bonds, rather than bank loans, were
the principal form of debt. In a study of ultimate returns to
bonds in default, Eichengreen and Portes make the interesting
discovery that on a random sample of 81 defaulted bonds held
to maturity, the internal rate of return was 5.4 percent for
sterling bonds (all of which were government guaranteed),
3.25 percent for government-guaranteed dollar bonds, and
0.72 percent for the total sample of fifty dollar-denominated
bonds, seventeen of which were not government guaranteed
(Eichengreen and Portes 1986, table 1.5). In other words, at the
end of the day, bondholders on average received the full value
of their principal on defaulted bonds, plus, in the case of
sterling bonds, an interest rate not very different from the
contractual interest; or, in the case of the dollar bonds, an
interest rate considerably below the contractual interest (which
was around 7 percent on foreign dollar issues), but a positive
rate of interest nevertheless.

This surprising finding must be qualified in two ways. First, during the periods of default, before settlements were worked out with the bondholders, bonds often traded at heavy discount to their face value. Under the circumstances, it was advantageous for the debtors to buy back their own bonds in the open market. The Foreign Bondholders Protective Council complained that "government estimates indicate that almost a dozen countries in default in service payments on their dollar bonds, most of them alleging as a reason for their default a lack of dollar exchange, have been able to find enough of that exchange to repatriate from 15 percent to 50 percent of their outstanding dollar issues" (Annual Report for 1939, pp.9–10). The council reported that thirteen countries with $1.8 billion in outstanding dollar debt had repurchased about 25 percent of their debt, with at least one debtor—apparently a municipality—buying back 83 percent of its debt. Presumably further purchases were made with the high export earnings during the Second World War. So it is only the bondholders who held to maturity who received their full principal with some interest.

Second, World War II interceded before many of the bonds were paid off under the rescheduling arrangements, and between 1929 and 1953 their real value (as measured by the U.S. GNP deflator) declined about 44 percent, so the final payments were made in dollars that had depreciated substantially in real terms. The same point applies with even greater force to sterling bonds. Of course, the real value of any debt incurred in the 1920s with maturities to the 1950s or later would have suffered this depreciation, not just bonds in default. Nonetheless, inflation reduced the real value of the debt, and thus helped to "solve" the debt problem of the 1930s. Moreover, the Second World War created a strong demand for exports of primary products, so export earnings were enlarged for those countries outside the war zone, notably those in Latin America.

Defaults by domestic borrowers occur frequently, especially in times of recession. Under Chapter 11 of the U.S. Bankruptcy Act, debtors who cannot service their debts can appeal for relief from their creditors while they reorganize their affairs, under court supervision, and work out satisfactory arrangements with their creditors. Such arrangements can entail virtually anything the debtor and a 67 percent majority of the creditors can agree on—including in practice deferment of principal repayment, reductions in interest rates, or swaps of debt for some form of equity in the company. Minority dissenting creditors are obliged to accept the arrangements, subject to certain conditions. Of course, sometimes no mutually satisfactory arrangement can be worked out between debtor and creditors, and the firm is then put into court-supervised receivership, for continued operation or liquidation. In other words, the old management is replaced and the firm continues to function under court supervision. If the receiver decides that the firm is not likely to become profitable, the firm is liquidated, its assets sold, and the proceeds distributed on a court-ordered formula among the creditors. This mechanism—roughly analogous ones exist in other countries—is designed to permit viable debtors to get back on their financial feet without being forced by their creditors to close and liquidate.

For obvious reasons, there can be no exact counterparts to this procedure when the debtors are sovereign nations, but the Paris and London Club procedures for rescheduling debt offer a rough analogy, with the International Monetary Fund playing the role of the court-appointed supervisor of the reorganization. The mechanisms for official debt relief were at first less varied than those in Chapter 11 proceedings, but in the late 1980s they began to show greater flexibility.

5   The Lingering Problem of Debt: Proposed Solutions

Soon after the eruption of the debt crisis in 1982, many proposals were put forward to deal with it.[1] Most were too vague to be useful, indicating that the author had not thought through the operational implications. Many of them, on close inspection, were aimed mainly at relieving the pressures on the world banking system, with little debt relief for debt-ridden countries. The viability of the banking system was of major concern in the early 1980s, but the relative burden on the banks of developing-country loans receded substantially by the late 1980s, and the remaining pressures on American banks arose from causes other than sovereign debt.

By the mid-to-late 1980s, therefore, proposals concerning international debt focused mainly on providing financial relief to debt-ridden countries, with a view to encouraging a resumption of their economic growth. These proposals can be organized under three broad headings: global debt relief, unilateral action by debtors, and a case-by-case approach.

An example of the global approach, in principle covering all indebted developing countries, would be the suggestion that debt service be limited to some measure of ability to pay, such as 20 percent of total export earnings, or that it be keyed to movements in a country's terms of trade.

A more complicated global solution was the suggestion by Senator William Bradley in 1986 that all official and bank creditors lower interest rates on outstanding debts by 3 percentage points for three years, and in addition reduce outstanding principal by 3 percent a year for three years. Furthermore, the multilateral development banks were to lend an additional $3 billion a year. Commercial banks would cease to be pressured into lending more to heavily indebted countries. The proposal was illustrated with the ten largest Latin American debtors, but was put forward as a basis for more general application. It was publicized widely and met with both strong approval and strong disapproval.[2]

All the global proposals suffer from a basic weakness, namely that they treat similarly countries with very different circumstances.[3] In general, they provide little or no relationship between the amount of debt relief and the payoff in terms of increased output and employment, or alleviation of poverty, or any other social condition in which we might be directly interested. Furthermore, debt relief on these global schemes will not reflect changing circumstances over time, except insofar as they are built into the formula. The year 1986, with sharply lower oil prices and interest rates, was very different from 1985—much better for Brazil and Korea, for instance, and worse for Mexico and Nigeria.

Moreover, these global schemes have some costs, mainly in terms of the loss of external influence in altering the policies of debtor nations so as to improve economic performance and maximize the prospect of ultimate debt repayment. Another cost is reduced voluntary lending to all developing countries for a longer period on grounds that violation of contracts on past debts presages possible violation of contracts on future debts. This last cost could be eliminated for some debtor countries by allowing them selectively to opt out of the scheme, although such an option would no doubt generate divisive debates within many debtor countries.

The proposal placing a ceiling on the debt-service ratio has some appeal, partly because it relates debt service to ability to pay, partly because it discriminates among countries in a relevant way, that is, those with low ratios, even if they have large debts, get no debt relief. But the proposal shares most of the general weaknesses of any global approach. In addition, it has little theoretical justification, because appropriate investments can make it possible and even desirable for a country to carry quite high debt-servicing ratios. Moreover, it neglects the fact that the export industries of different countries depend differentially on imported inputs. Thus Mexico, with its substantial border-zone processing industry, would be penalized relative to, say, Argentina, whose exports have fewer imported inputs. This weakness could be remedied by putting the same ceiling on the ratio of debt service to *value added* in exports. But that would both complicate the scheme and introduce a source of unproductive disputation, for ex-

ample, over whether domestic inputs in direct competition
with imported inputs should be included.

If global solutions are not likely to be feasible or desirable,
what about the alternative of unilateral actions? Debtor countries know best their own problems, and in particular the
political and local economic costs of continuing to service their
heavy debts. If these costs become too great, they can simply
stop servicing the debts, or they can service them selectively
or partially.

Unilateral action to restrict debt payment has serious potential
costs. Financial assets could be frozen, with serious consequences for normal trade, as Iran discovered in early 1980.
Trade credits could dry up. Physical assets such as aircraft or
cargoes could be seized abroad in payment of debt (provided
the assets belonged to the actual debtor—the government—
not to some resident of the debtor country). These actions
would force trade onto a cash-and-carry basis, which for some
countries would be difficult and costly and indeed would
cause a sharp drop in GNP due to a loss of crucial imported
inputs.[4]

These are extreme possibilities, likely to arise only if a country
repudiates its external debt. As Kaletsky (1985) points out,
some of these actions are not legally easy, and they have
potential costs for the creditors as well as for the debtor. So
long as debtors are making a plausible effort to repay, creditors are not likely to engage in attachments or other extreme
actions, and a skillful debtor will continue to keep his ongoing
trade credits up to date, even if his uncovered bank loans fall

into arrears. So long as debtors seem to be making an effort, have a plausible story for not being able to do more, and hold out some prospect for better times ahead, they will probably avoid the worst costs beyond the drying up of new uncovered credits.

Partly for nonfinancial reasons, partly because of uncertainties about creditor response, and partly because there is at least a hope of getting new credits to cover the relevant portion of interest payments, debtor nations usually prefer a third course: negotiation with leading creditors. Much is made of the "case-by-case" approach, but it now takes place in a framework that has been well established and much used. The framework provides common procedures, but with different outcomes depending on individual circumstances, subject however to the influence of past precedents and concern about setting future precedents.

The procedure involves an initiation by the debtor of a so-called Paris Club meeting of its governmental creditors (including claims guaranteed by the creditor governments).[5] These have been occurring since the mid-1960s, but rose in frequency from one or two a year to a peak of twenty-one in 1985 and an average of sixteen a year in 1986–88. The debtor presents to the creditors its situation and prospects as it sees them. The IMF staff is typically also asked to produce an independent report. Creditors decide on the nature of debt relief that is appropriate—the period of debt covered, the maturity and grace period for the rescheduled debt and interest due, the coverage of rescheduling, and occasionally the concessions with respect to interest rates. The debtor stipulates that other creditors, other than the international financial institutions, will not be treated more favorably than those present. The creation of this general framework is followed by a series of bilateral negotiations with official creditors, whether they were at the Paris Club or not. Creditors may include the Soviet Union or other East European countries, OPEC countries, or even other developing countries, such as Venezuela or Brazil. Governments from the OECD countries account for only 19 percent of total Sub-Saharan African debt, for example (World Bank 1986, p.81).

The Paris Club for official creditors has its parallel for private bank creditors in the "London Club." One or a few lead creditor banks chair an "advisory committee" of large bank creditors that negotiates with the debtor terms for new loans or for rescheduling outstanding loans. The banks then undertake to persuade other bank creditors—which may number several hundred—to agree to the negotiated package. This is often an arduous and time-consuming process.

Both Paris and London Club negotiations are typically keyed to a satisfactory IMF program in the debtor country, so the country undertakes negotiations with the IMF for a one- or three-year program. As discussed in chapter 2, under the program the IMF puts up some money and the country agrees to certain policy actions, which at a minimum involve restraints on domestic credit creation and on the budget deficit. These actions often also involve a change in the exchange rate and in interest rates and perhaps a ceiling on new foreign borrowing. The point of the program is to get the economy on to a viable path that is not excessively dependent on new and generally unavailable external borrowing.

Finally, as noted in chapter 2, the World Bank has increasingly been engaged as a source of nonproject funds and policy advice involving longer-term structural features of the economy, such as agricultural or energy policy. In this connection it makes so-called structural adjustment loans.

The full record of these arrangements is not outstanding. Many IMF programs do not stick and need to be renegotiated, and perhaps renegotiated again. That outcome does not necessarily mean that the arrangement has failed completely, however, especially if circumstances have changed in a substantial way, as they frequently have in recent years. The main impact of the arrangements is to postpone amortization of debts coming due. In this respect, the procedure is like a Chapter 11 reorganization, but until 1989 with less flexibility in terms of both concessions by creditors and demands on debtors, which are sovereign nations. Late in the decade the international financial institutions together with the governments of several rich countries introduced a number of "enhancements," which encouraged commercial banks to offer debt relief beyond rescheduling.

A standard complaint is that the IMF squeezes debtor nations too severely and possibly in the wrong ways. This may be correct. The IMF is not perfect, and it is subject to its own doctrine. But the IMF is charged with designing a plausible and viable program within the constraints set by what it can do, and by what it can plausibly ask creditors to do. It does not always have enough funds for its task—its request for a 100 percent increase in quotas was turned down in 1983, in favor of a 50 percent increase two years later. That being said, the IMF does not use all of the funds at its disposal.[6] It has no authority to write down the value of outstanding debt. It can only encourage postponement of debt amortization and request new loans, both of which it has done, country by country.

The Baker Plan and the Brady Initiative

In September 1985 Treasury secretary James Baker put forward a plan designed to ease the debt problems of developing countries and at the same time to improve their economic performance. He identified fifteen countries heavily indebted to commercial banks[7] and suggested that commercial banks and multilateral development banks (MDBs) together should increase their lending to these countries by nearly $30 billion over the following three years, in exchange for structural reforms in the macroeconomic and allocative policies of the debt-ridden countries. Of the new loans, the commercial banks were asked to put up $20 billion.

The key premise of the Baker Plan was that debtor countries were in a temporary liquidity (foreign exchange) crisis and that a concerted injection of funds combined with policy reforms would lead to a resumption of truly voluntary bank lending. This premise turned out to be false. Most banks felt overexposed with developing-country debt and desired to reduce their outstanding claims, even under somewhat improved circumstances. In the event, total commercial bank claims on Latin America and Africa fell by $15 billion between the end of 1985 and the end of 1988, the period of the Baker Plan (and they fell by another $30 billion in 1989).[8] It is true that a reduction in debt of nearly $16 billion was achieved through debt-equity swaps, whereby the banks exchanged or sold debt claims for various equity interests within the debtor countries. It is also true, as William Cline has pointed out, that the banks together advanced $13 billion to the fifteen countries through new money plans, representing about two-thirds of Secretary Baker's target. But despite that their total claims declined significantly.

In March 1989 the new U.S. Treasury Secretary, Nicholas Brady, signaled a change in U.S. policy, for the first time endorsing a reduction of commercial bank debt (the 1988 Toronto economic summit had already agreed that official development loans to the poorest countries should be written off), but on a voluntary basis. More important, Brady also suggested that IMF lending need not be conditioned on a rescheduling agreement between debtor countries and their commercial bank creditors.

During the next eighteen months agreements were reached between Mexico, the Philippines, Costa Rica, and Venezuela and their commercial bank creditors under the Brady initiative. Of these, the most important quantitatively and in terms of possible precedent was that with Mexico. Mexico initially requested the equivalent in new loans, debt reduction, or interest-rate reduction of 55 percent of its annual interest payments on about $50 billion of long-term debt to commercial banks. A package was signed in early 1990 that gave commercial banks a choice between (1) increasing loans by 25 percent over four years, (2) exchanging claims for thirty-year bonds with a fixed interest rate of 6.25 percent (down from floating rates running around 10 percent), or (3) converting claims into thirty-year bonds at floating rates carrying a face value of 65 percent of the claims so converted. Both types of bonds would be fully guaranteed through collateral (zero-coupon U.S., Japanese, and European treasury bonds), and the interest on them would be guaranteed for eighteen months, so the debt or interest rate reduction by the banks would be made in exchange for a sounder asset.

Mexican officials expected that about 60 percent of the debt would be converted to the discounted "exit bonds" (so named because they would be marketable and holders would be relieved from participation in any future rescheduling), 20 percent to the lower-interest-rate bonds, and 20 percent in new loans. In the event, few banks elected to make new loans, perhaps because of ever stiffer reserve requirements that bank regulators in many creditor countries were imposing on all loans to debt-ridden developing countries. Nearly 90 percent elected exit bonds, of which 42 percent were in discount bonds and 47 percent were in reduced-interest bonds. Mexican officials reckoned that the package saved Mexico about $4 billion in debt-service payments each year from 1991 through 1994 (*Financial Times*, March 30, 1990).[9] The international community was involved not only in encouraging the banks to engage in debt reduction but also in advancing most of the funds for purchasing the collateral and guaranteeing the interest payments.

The difficulty of reaching agreement with respect to Mexico, the relatively small (but not inconsequential) reduction in debt, and the relatively few banks that elected to provide new money all suggest that the Brady approach falls far short of what many developing countries consider necessary to resume a net flow of resources adequate for growth and development, and of what U.S. Treasury officials originally forecast. Moreover, the bankers involved were reluctant to repeat the Mexican process with other countries, although Costa Rica, the Philippines, and Venezuela were able to reach agreements that involved some debt reduction.[10] As of the end of the 1980s, in short, banks were not prepared to make major concessions to debtors on the terms available to them, and public authorities felt that they had reached their limit in "enhancements" in the Mexican case. Thus the "debt problem" was still unsolved.

The Kenen Proposal

Yet by the end of the 1980s there seemed to be room for a mutually advantageous "deal" among the three relevant parties: the debtor countries, the commercial banks, and the governments of the rich countries where the commercial bank creditors resided. The stockholders of the banks were clearly suffering from depressed market values of their shares, in part because of the heavy weight of nonperforming developing-country loans in bank portfolios. Reducing those portfolios would, on the right terms, improve their position. The debtor countries were struggling to reduce budget deficits and improve trade positions in the face of heavy debt-servicing requirements, and obviously any reduction in their obligations could, in a context of appropriate policies, contribute to the resumption of economic growth. Finally, the taxpayers of the rich countries were suffering because of the low actual and prospective tax payments by the large banks, and because low demand in developing countries implied lower demand for their products, lower export growth, and possibly lower overall growth. It should be possible to put these three conditions together into a mutually beneficial package.

One proposal that attempts to do this has been made by Peter Kenen of Princeton University.[11] He has suggested the creation of an International Debt Discount Corporation (IDDC) which, like the World Bank, would issue public bonds that would be guaranteed by the major industrial countries. The proceeds of those bonds would be used to buy, for cash, selective commercial bank claims on developing countries, at a price equal to 50 to 60 percent of the face value of debt—a price well above quotations in the (thin) secondary market for such claims, but well below face value. The IDDC in turn would reduce servicing requirements on these claims by a nearly corresponding amount, after allowing for building a contingency reserve in the IDDC.

The net effect of these transactions would be to relieve commercial banks of the tendered debt in exchange for cash or high-quality bonds, to reduce by 40 percent or more the debt service on the tendered debt, and to leave governments of the rich countries with a contingent obligation should something go badly wrong, but with a net gain if, as expected, the scheme was successful. The gain would be measured not only in more vigorous and efficient growth in the world economy, but actually in financial return once (many years later) the IDDC could be liquidated and its reserve and net earnings be repatriated to the sponsoring nations.

Kenen would have debtor countries declare whether or not they wished their claims to be involved in the scheme, and then commercial banks would decide how much of their claims (if any) they wished to tender, on the condition that they tender claims on all participating debtor countries in a basket, to avoid adverse selection. But bank participation would be voluntary. Kenen argues that this arrangement would increase the total value of the bank claims that remain outstanding. In other words, some countries are so burdened with commercial bank debt that the total expected value of the debt to creditors would rise by writing off a substantial portion of the debt. This contention is doubtful, at least for the major Latin American countries, but it is not necessary to make the proposal attractive.[12] It is perhaps the most sensible of the various global proposals that have been put forward. Although it suffers from some of the weaknesses inherent to global solutions mentioned above, eligibility of access to the facility could be limited to those developing countries meeting stiff criteria initially.

In any case, it is not likely to be realized. The basic problem is that the cash price required by the banks to relinquish voluntarily their claims in a volume large enough to be helpful to the debt-ridden countries in 1990 is probably still substantially higher than the price the taxpaying publics of the rich countries are willing to advance to them.[13] There are several reasons for this.

First, all the industrial countries are feeling some fiscal pressure and desire to reduce rather than increase government financial commitments. Although guarantees avoid a direct fiscal outlay, they create a contingent liability.

Second, at least in the United States, considerable skepticism about the "low cost" of guarantees exists in view of the large cost of the bailout of the savings and loan institutions, whose depositors enjoyed a government guarantee. Moreover, this concern is not without merit at the international level, as governments have already agreed to write off remaining foreign aid loans to the poorest (mainly African) countries, and they are being requested to extend write-offs both to other claims on the poorest countries and to middle-income countries, such as Poland.

Third, although at Kenen's proposed discount of 40 to 50 percent banks are hardly being "bailed out," bank stockholders would very likely benefit from the arrangement, and that would not be politically attractive in view of the widespread sentiment that banks were at least partly responsible for the debt problem.

Fourth, and perhaps most compelling, parliamentary debate over the creation of the IDDC would focus attention on the large volume of private capital that the residents of the debtor nations moved out of their countries during the late 1970s and early 1980s. It is in the nature of such capital that no hard figures are available, and dispute has been vigorous over estimates of "capital flight" derived from the residuals of balance-of-payments data. The United Nations (1986) provided a calculation for the period 1981–84, that is, including data from only a year and a half before the debt crisis erupted. They estimate unrecorded capital movements of $31 billion from Mexico, $13 billion from Argentina, and $3 billion from Brazil over this period. Lessard and Williamson (1987) provide a more comprehensive assessment over a longer period. They estimate total capital flight from four Latin American debtor nations of $82 billion during the period 1976–84. There is little dispute that the numbers for some countries are very large. Taxpayers of the industrialized democracies will be reluctant to take financial responsibility for debts whose counterpart assets remain untouched in the ownership of residents of debtor nations. At a minimum, they will want to be assured that the earnings on these investments are properly taxed, and at a maximum they will want to see much of the capital repatriated as a condition for any debt relief. This is a potential political problem of some magnitude.[14]

Prospects for the Future

At the end of the day, some countries will be unable realistically to service their debts. There are two possible problems. The first is that debt-service requirements are simply too large for a country's net exports to cover at current world prices, given its crucial import requirements. With extensive development, the country might eventually be able to service its current level of debt. But that would require yet additional investment and restructuring of the economy. Past debt has in effect been squandered, either for consumption (including public consumption, such as spending for the armed forces) or because the investments it made were ill-conceived or turned out not to be productive. Under these circumstances, once expenditure has been reduced to what the country can produce, continued servicing of past debts may be a poor use of output by anyone's standard. The countries subject to these conditions are largely in Africa.

The second possible problem, quite different in character, is that *governments* have taken on greater debt than their effective taxing capacity, in the sense that higher tax rates will result in lower revenue and a lower ability to service debt. This problem may have arisen because of government assumption at some point of the external debt of private enterprises. If, for example, maximum taxing capacity is 10 percent of GDP, as it may be in some very poor countries, the government cannot feasibly service an external debt at the rate of 10 percent of GDP.

There is a serious interaction between these two problems, in that depreciation of the currency is often seen as a step toward generating the additional export revenue required to service the external debts. But currency depreciation also increases proportionately the local currency requirement for servicing a given foreign-currency debt and thus increases government expenditure. The oft-recommended solution to the net export problem—currency devaluation—therefore may worsen the tax capacity problem. Where the limits of taxing capacity are reached, some form of debt write-down, direct or indirect, is necessary.

Various strategies are possible:

1. There can be a formal write-off of enough debt by both official and private creditors to make servicing the remaining debt a viable proposition. This write-down might take place indirectly, for example, through acceptance by creditors of blocked local currency payments that can only be invested within the country. The local use of such accounts will be inflationary to the extent that the government borrows from the central bank to make the payments rather than taxing the public.

2. A foreign benefactor may appear who pays down the debt or gives enough aid to release export earnings to pay down the debt.

3. Creditors could help debtors in capturing resident capital abroad, which may be used to repay part of the foreign debt, or to tax interest earnings on such capital, thus helping to defray interest charges on debt.

4. Debtors could scale back their payments of interest to their own assessment of ability to pay and allow arrears to rise.

It is perhaps worth noting how this problem is handled domestically. Nonpayment of debt forces bankruptcy, and if a bankrupt firm cannot be reorganized in a way to make it viable, it is put into receivership, at which time the stockholders lose their stake and management is replaced. These two developments reduce the moral hazard of easy movement into bankruptcy. That course of action is not possible for countries, although in earlier times creditors sometimes took over directly the collection of customs and other revenues. The problem of moral hazard could be addressed at an international level by attempting to establish the principle that any country given a write-down in its external debt would be required to make payment in some form of "equity" such as foreign ownership of a part of its state enterprises, or partial claims on customs revenue, or local currency investment in export industries with the promise of future transfer of any future earnings.[15] These are sensitive issues, touching on national sovereignty. And in today's world it may not be possible to move forcefully in this direction.

With developing-country debt trading at substantial discount in secondary markets, an apparently attractive and inexpensive way to reduce the debt would be for the debtor country to purchase its debt at the discounted prices and retire it. The problem with this solution concerns the source of funds for the purchase of the debt. It is awkward, to say the least, for a country that claims inability to service its external debt to nonetheless find sufficient funds to purchase debt in the secondary market. Creditors will rightly consider that foul play, particularly since the discount is governed by the apparent ability and willingness of the debtor to service its debts. It would brand the debtor untrustworthy for long in the future. Consortium loan agreements typically prohibit such action by the debtor, so to avoid formal violation of the loan agreements requires a waiver by the creditors, which they are unlikely to give in the absence of substantial "enhancements" as part of an overall debt-reduction package.

Alternatively, the international community—ultimately the taxpayers of the rich countries—can provide the funds for the buybacks. But there are several disadvantages to this approach. First, the discounts are largest on debts not currently being serviced and with no immediate prospect for being serviced. Purchasing such debts, for the same reason, provides no actual relief to the debtor country. Second, a *policy* of buyback on a scale sufficient to make a significant difference to the debtor will itself bid up the secondary market price (i.e., reduce the market discount), making the policy more expensive relative to the gains.

Third, for the same reason, large creditors are likely to withhold their claims from the secondary market if they see some significant prospect of restoring their full value, so again the policy is likely to be limited in its effects. Despite these various objections, a policy of buyback may be of some limited value in an overall debt-reduction package, as it was for the Philippines, in providing a useful way of buying out small creditors that are unwilling to participate in future debt restructuring deals, particulary if new loans are expected to be made.

The international community can nonetheless undertake a number of ameliorative steps, aimed not directly at the debt problem but at the broader problem of economic development, which heavy debt burdens aggravate.[16] First, we could have an allocation of SDRs by the IMF. There have only been two such allocations, one starting in 1970 and the second in 1979. An SDR allocation goes to all members of the IMF, and developing countries receive about 30 percent of it. A plausible allocation would not make a major dent in total external debt, but it would relieve somewhat the cash-flow problems of many developing countries and would be desirable in its own right to keep the SDR alive, even if it falls short of the international commitment of 1976 to make the SDR the centerpiece of the international monetary system.

Second, there could continue to be generous replenishments of IDA, which transfers resources to the poorest countries, some of whom are burdened by debt-servicing obligations. In December 1989 the leading donors agreed on an IDA replenishment amounting to $15 billion over three years. Again, the object is not to offer debt relief but to provide resources that contribute to the overall economic development of the poorest countries.

Third, the IMF could once again sell off a portion of its large gold holdings for a substantial capital gain. At the end of 1989 the IMF held 103 million ounces of gold, carried on its books at a value of SDR 3.6 billion. The gold is a legacy of historical subscriptions by member countries; its book value was the equivalent of $4.7 billion. The market value of this gold at the end of 1989 was $41.1 billion. The gold is not essential to IMF operations and serves no socially useful function. A number of poor countries remain in arrears with the IMF, which impedes other relations with the IMF and with the international financial community more generally. By selling less than 20 percent of the gold, the IMF could raise enough profits to rectify the arrears of poor countries with new, low-interest loans, and to contribute additional resources to the IMF trust fund for subsidizing interest rates on other advances to poor countries, or to finance purchases of debt that trades at heavy discount in the secondary market. (The trust fund was created with the profits from IMF gold sales following the first oil shock in the mid-1970s.)

Fourth, in the absence of sufficient new and appropriately usable funds, it may be necessary to reschedule the debts of the multilateral development banks (MDBs) in low-income countries. Debt to these institutions accounts for nearly a quarter of the total debt of Sub-Saharan Africa, and in some cases it is difficult to imagine useful debt rescheduling that does not include the multilateral development credits. Such claims have been exempt from rescheduling, and that is certainly desirable if possible. But it would be better to reschedule these debts than to cripple the development prospects of some developing countries. The creditworthiness of the multilateral development banks, contrary to what is sometimes claimed, would not suffer if their debts were rescheduled, because that creditworthiness rests principally on the guarantees of the MDB bonds extended by the industrialized countries rather than on the quality of the MDB portfolio of assets.[17] Of course, it would be unnecessary to reschedule if new MDB nonproject lending were sufficiently high to cover the costs of servicing outstanding MDB debt. It must be emphasized that rescheduling or other forms of debt relief can be truly helpful only if reinforced by the appropriate policies in the debtor country; where such policies are in place, the MDBs have generally been willing to lend enough to avoid rescheduling their outstanding debt.

Fifth, the industrial countries should stand ready to help, mainly through providing information, in enforcing taxes on income and assets held abroad by residents of developing countries that have serious debt-servicing problems. They could go even further and encourage the debt-ridden countries to step up their tax-enforcement efforts and to request such assistance.

These would be useful ameliorative steps, but none of them separately nor all of them together represent a full solution. Nonetheless, many countries are slowly growing out of the debt problem. It has been an unnecessarily painful process, but it is occurring. The most likely outcome is that this process will continue, abetted as in the past by selective nonpayment of interest on outstanding debt, allowing arrears to build.[18] The interest due on debt in effect provides a line of credit that governments can draw on as needed; in good times—for example, when export earnings and tax revenues are exceptionally high—the arrears can be reduced. They can be further reduced through periodic debt reschedulings that capitalize them. As table 5.1 demonstrates, the combination of arrears

Table 5.1
Impact on interest payments of reschedulings and arrears (as a percentage of exports of goods and services)

	Fifteen highly indebted countries	Sub-Saharan Africa
1979–81	-0.1	1.9
1982	0.8	2.7
1983	0.9	3.5
1984	1.6	6.2
1985	1.6	4.6
1986	2.7	8.3
1987	5.0	10.0
1988	2.3	10.6

Note: Comparison is between scheduled interest payments before rescheduling and actual interest payments.
Source: Group of Ten, *The Role of the IMF and the World Bank in the Context of the Debt Strategy*, June 1989.

and rescheduling has resulted in substantial and progressively larger reductions in interest payments from those originally scheduled, especially in Sub-Saharan Africa. Rescheduling and arrears of course involve refinancing rather than debt reduction.

The international community took the critical step in 1989, following Brady's initiative, of divorcing IMF, World Bank, and other official lending from the condition that formal arrangements be in place between debtor country and commercial bank creditors before disbursement could take place. While resented by the banks, this step was obviously necessary, since the preceding conditional arrangement unwittingly strengthened the position of the commercial banks at the debt negotiations and resulted in delays that were often so long that changes in the underlying economic conditions nullified the terms of the IMF/World Bank program to which the debtor country had agreed. The IMF should not be or appear to be the debt collector for the commercial banks. A credible IMF program will improve the prospects for debt servicing, but should do so by improving the prospects for the economy of the debtor country. Critical imports must take precedence over payment of interest, if new loans cannot be arranged.

In short, the world will pursue a course of muddling through, and in general it will probably work. Some of the African countries mark an exception: there the level of debt has reached such proportions that there is no reasonable hope that it can be repaid, even on easier terms. Many African countries have acute fundamental problems of development and even governance, and external debt is a relatively minor contribution to those problems. No doubt in the end there will be substantial reduction of debt, most of which is official; in the meantime those countries have allowed their arrears to build. Their position with the IMF can be rectified through the sale of IMF gold, as noted above.

Apart from specific help to individual debtor countries under suitable conditions, the industrialized countries are responsible for the overall tone of the world economy. In the context of the debt problem, it is especially important that reasonable growth in markets for the exports of developing countries occur, so that their export growth can exceed interest rates, a necessary condition for declining debt-to-export ratios. That in turn requires reasonable economic growth in the industrialized countries, and it requires that the industrialized countries maintain their markets free from serious protection. Signs in 1990 were ambiguous on both scores. With the United States moving toward fiscal contraction, other leading countries should engage in some expansion, and the Federal Reserve should ease short-term interest rates. Both the United States and the European Community have drifted toward greater import protection, as both the U.S. administration and the Brussels Commission attempt to buy off even more severe protection proposed by the U.S. Congress or by national governments in Europe. Japan to be sure moved in the opposite direction, but at a glacial speed. So the industrialized countries cannot rest comfortably on the assumption that the mere passage of time will solve the problem.

In the end, the debt problem will be solved by some combination of negotiated settlement and unilateral action. Debtor countries will have to judge for themselves whether the squeeze that results from a negotiated settlement either threatens their political system or goes beyond what they deem to be fruitful in producing structural reforms. To the extent that the world market for developing countries' exports slumps, we are likely to see a greater resort to unilateral action and a lower reliance on negotiated settlement.

Notes

Introduction

1. See, for example, Schultze and Lawrence 1987.

2. I owe a great deal to my collaborators in that study, W. M. Corden, I. M. D. Little, and S. Rajapatirana, as well as the more numerous authors of country studies, for many stimulating conversations and exchanges of information. I have drawn liberally on their ideas in presenting my own, but I remain solely responsible for the interpretations offered here.

Chapter 1

1. In the United States, the price of gasoline in real terms in the late 1980s was about the same as it was in 1973. But this was due to the decline in the real value of gasoline taxes; world crude oil prices, adjusted for inflation, remained nearly twice what they were in 1973, even after the declines of the 1980s.

2. The dynamics of the second oil price increase differed radically from those of the first, with OPEC posted prices following the rise in the spot market over two years.

3. At the time, OPEC was not a cartel in the standard sense, as it did not attempt to control the output of its members, only the price at which they sold. OPEC did not become a cartel until it introduced agreed production quotas in 1982.

4. Most economic data reported for developing countries should be regarded as hypotheses rather than facts. They represent someone's best guess about what happened. One of the frustrations for anyone analyzing these economies is not simply the paucity of data in some instances, but the inconsistencies among different sources even when the sources are all from the same national government. For instance, the change in the terms of trade reported in the *International Financial Statistics* of the International Monetary Fund often differ significantly from those in the data base of the World Bank, being significantly worse in 1973–74 for Kenya and Thailand than the figures reported in table 1.2, and significantly better for Brazil, Morocco, Sri Lanka, and Turkey.

I have relied largely on statistics made available by the International Monetary Fund and the World Bank, because they are accessible to readers and broadly consistent across countries; where they differ I have used the series that covers the most countries. But all figures should be treated as rough indicators of what occurred, not exact measurements.

5. Again, *International Financial Statistics* (IFS) shows different figures for changes in the terms of trade over the period 1978–81, in this case substantially worse than the figures reported in table 1.5 for India, Kenya, Pakistan, and Sri Lanka, by amounts that vary from 5 percentage points (India) to 13.5 percentage points (Kenya).

6. Cameroon shows a deterioration in the terms of trade, which is due no doubt to the sharp fall in coffee and cocoa prices between 1978 and 1981. The sharp increase in oil prices is underrepresented because Cameroon oil exports were growing rapidly during this period and were negligible in 1978. Moreover, the deterioration in the current account may be more apparent than real, since Cameroon oil-export revenues are a state secret, and some of them were systematically sequestered abroad.

7. This measurement is the IMF concept, which is an own-country trade-weighted movement of nominal exchange rates with the cur-

rencies of its leading trade partners, corrected for differential movements in wholesale prices in those same countries.

8. Lessard and Williamson (1987) estimated that $16 billion left the country between 1976 and 1984, but most flight occurred in 1979–81.

9. Many countries devalued their currencies in the early 1980s, however, and that alone increased the value of external debt relative to GDP without any additional borrowing. If this factor is allowed for, eight countries increased their debt-to-GDP ratio by more than 5 percentage points between 1978 and 1983, and seven did so in the period 1973–78.

10. The special drawing right is a synthetic international unit of account that represents a weighted average of five leading currencies: the U.S. dollar, Japanese yen, British pound, German mark, and French franc.

11. Because it was first clearly identified with the discovery and development of large reserves of natural gas in the Netherlands in the late 1950s and early 1960s.

12. Unless the goods are protected against imports by quotas or other nontariff barriers. For a clear exposition of the Dutch disease effects, see Corden and Neary 1982. These effects are not limited to developing countries. Britain's development of North Sea oil in the early 1980s, combined with the macroeconomic policies of Britain, depressed British manufacturing industry; and the substantial capital inflow into the United States in the early 1980s, leading to a strong appreciation of the dollar, had a similar impact.

13. Increased investment in the form of construction would be expected to draw labor from other activities and to put upward pressure on real wages, but our countries do not have adequate data on wages to make meaningful comparisons.

Chapter 2

1. Because of the sharp change in relative prices between tradables and nontradables and between oil and all other goods and services that occurred during the 1980s, it will not be surprising to discover that GDP growth during this decade is revised upward in many developing countries as more recent prices are used for the calculation of real GDP.

2. P is sometimes confusingly called the "real exchange rate" in the professional economic literature, but it bears only a rough relationship to the commonly used measurement of the real exchange rate based on actual exchange rates adjusted by relative changes in overall national price levels.

3. Choosing imports as the unit of measurement is appropriate with respect to the country's external position and relation to the rest of the world, but the decline in welfare must also take into account the consumption of nontraded goods and services. Among our countries, domestic production (and consumption) of nontraded goods and services actually fell in Chile in 1973–75 and in Brazil, Chile, Costa Rica, and Nigeria in 1978–83.

Internally consistent data required to undertake a full decomposition of effects along the lines of equation (2) are not available for most countries.

4. Over the period 1975–85 the central governments of a sample of twenty-four developing countries financed 8.3 percent of their deficits from nonbank domestic sources, 38.3 percent from external sources, and 53.6 percent from the banking system (of which 46.7 percentage points were directly from the central bank). See World Bank 1990, p. 62.

5. But they may have entailed other restrictions, regarding, for example, the purpose for which the funds could be used or where they could be spent. Some countries preferred bank loans, despite the higher charges, because of the greater freedom they permitted.

6. The World Bank typically makes loans for specific projects, such as building dams or ports or rural road networks, and the disbursement takes place over the many years of construction. The SALs could be disbursed more quickly and also got the World Bank involved in policy formulation to a much greater extent. In both respects, they resembled the program loans of the 1960s. See Asher and Mason 1973.

7. There are some exceptions. Cameroon and the Ivory Coast belong to currency unions in which the countries have some voice in money creation, but not a determining one. And until the late 1980s Liberia and Panama both used the U.S. dollar as their domestic currency, so residents had to earn their currency through exporting. Hong Kong has a currency board, which issues Hong Kong dollars only in exchange for foreign currency.

8. The inflation tax arises also from the increased demand by commercial banks for bank reserves, insofar as these do not receive a market rate of interest, which is the case in most countries. The inflation tax is sometimes also applied to outstanding bonds. But, as noted, the nonbank market for bonds is limited in most developing countries, and some of that is compulsory, so the holders are not likely to increase voluntarily their bond holdings in order to maintain their real value. Marketable bonds that are purchased voluntarily must in general command an interest rate that reflects the expected rate of inflation.

9. Over half of the value of outstanding U.S. currency is in the form of $100 bills, a total of $115 billion at the end of 1989. These bills are rarely seen in ordinary transactions in the United States, and the drug trade and other illegal activities cannot plausibly account for more than about one-third of them. Many of them are known to be abroad, especially in countries with high rates of inflation or with tight controls on foreign exchange.

10. There is little available evidence on cash holdings by income class in developing countries or on the incidence of the inflation tax. Gil-

Diaz (1987) estimates that for Mexico in 1980 the greatest incidence of the inflation tax fell on the highest-income decile of the population, at 6.8 percent of income. The next greatest incidence fell on the lowest-income decile, at 6.6 percent of income. The least incidence fell on the fourth (from bottom) decile, at 2.2 percent of income, with the incidence generally rising as incomes rose or fell from this decile. His estimates allow for bank balances (including corporate balances imputed to ultimate owners) as well as currency. Gil-Diaz expresses some surprise at the relatively high levels of currency held by the lowest-income decile, but indicates that they are consistent with an income-expenditure survey.

11. Of course, higher inflation will also impinge on the real value of government spending, insofar as budgets are not increased enough to make full allowance for the inflation that actually takes place. Real revenues are also affected, insofar as the real value of regular tax collections diminishes because collections lag behind the income or sales subject to the tax. But this Oliviera-Tanzi effect should not be exaggerated, because governments in countries with a history of high inflation have typically geared tax collections to the inflationary environment, for example, by requiring quick payment or sometimes even advance payment of taxes.

12. The latter was rarer in developing countries, as they usually control deposit rates and thus insulate deposit banks to some extent from changes in real interest rates. Chile was the major exception.

13. Most of these financial crises were resolved with heavy support, direct or indirect, from the central bank, sometimes but not always after the management of the financial institutions in difficulty was changed. In Korea, for instance, low-interest loans from the Bank of Korea were made to deposit money banks to help them carry nonperforming loans to failed or shaky enterprises; and in Chile the central bank directly assumed some of the nonperforming debt as part of a capital restructuring of the financial institutions in difficulty.

14. Joan Nelson has argued that developing countries have been shortsighted in blaming the IMF, because it casts doubt on the ability of the government to defend the country's national interests. It might work once, but not repeatedly. She urges governments to take responsibility for their stabilization policies and then claim credit for getting the IMF's agreement. See "The Politics of Stabilization," in Feinberg and Kallab 1984.

15. The best recent example of extreme public skepticism can be found in Argentina, where there have been so many failed programs that a new program is greeted with extreme doubt. On the other hand, the doubt is sometimes mingled, once again, with hope. See de Pablo in Williamson 1990.

16. See the discussion by Dornbusch in Bossons et al. 1986 of the correction of the German hyperinflation of 1923, or that of Bolivia in 1985 by Cariaga in Williamson 1990. In Germany, judgment on the program was suspended for several months and was followed by a favorable swing in opinion, reflected in the movement of the forward exchange rate of the mark.

Appendix

1. Of course, if for some reason the country were initially producing at Q_2 that is, off the schedule QQ where resources are fully employed, it might not be necessary to endure a decline in production of N-goods. The reasons for the initial unemployment of resources must be known in order to analyze the changes that would need to be made.

2. This proposition holds even in the absence of negative externalities such as pollution or other undesirable environmental effects, which have been emphasized increasingly in recent years in criticizing GDP or GNP as a proxy for welfare.

It is noteworthy that at the prices prevailing at Q_1, GDP is higher than at Q_0. Because of the sharp change in relative prices between tradables and nontradables and between oil and all other goods and services that occurred during the 1980s, it will not be surprising to discover that GDP growth during this decade is revised upward in many developing countries as more recent prices are used for the calculation of real GDP.

Chapter 3

1. I use the real increase in GDP as the best all-around measure of economic growth. That determines a country's material standard of living in the long run. Real spending can deviate from that in the short run in response to changes in the terms of trade or to the possibility of borrowing abroad. Real GDP can increase for a time at the expense of the environment, but as per capita income grows, people are likely to become more sensitive to questions of air and water quality and to devote some of their increased output to improving and preserving that quality.

2. Indeed, the correlation between the total external shock—terms of trade plus interest on external debt, relative to GDP—over the period 1979–81 and growth during the 1980s was negative, implying a shock *helps* growth, but it was not statistically significant.

3. Inflation during the period 1965–80 provides no statistical explanation for growth in the 1980s. For the entire period 1965–88, the correlation between inflation and growth is -.59, a number statistically different from zero; but this result is determined entirely by two high-inflation, low-growth countries, Argentina and Chile. Without them, inflation is neither statistically nor economically significant as an explanatory variable.

4. Korea had an inflation rate (measured by the consumer price index) lower than that in the United States during the years 1984–88, but that was exceptional.

5. Technically, the measure of inflation variation is the standard error of an equation that estimates the trend rate of inflation over the period 1980–88.

6. The term *relatively* must be strongly emphasized here, because Korea, for example, could not in the 1970s be considered an open economy by the standards of industrialized countries. But it was more open and had devoted much greater attention to developing its export capacity than many other developing countries.

7. Balassa (1989) found that developing countries with outward-oriented policies as a group performed signlficantly better following both oil shocks than did those with inward-oriented policies. His generalizations are based on the group performance of nine countries (including four of our eighteen) in the former category and fifteen countries (including six of the eighteen) in the latter category.

Where countries covered overlap, Balassa classifies their policies the same as I do. But by looking only at group averages, he fails to note the significant exceptions to his generalizations.

8. I owe much of this and the following discussion to Ian Little.

9. When the degree of import compression and the variation in the real exchange rate are introduced as explanatory variables for trend economic growth during the 1980s, the trend inflation rate and variations around that trend lose what limited influence they had as explanatory variables. The two former variables account for about 56 percent of the variation in growth rates across our eighteen countries, both with high statistical significance, and the inflation variables, singly or together, do not contribute any further explanatory power.

10. The budget deficit or surplus reported here is that of the central government—that is, it excludes the deficits or surpluses of state and local governments, even though expenditures by these entities are extremely important in some countries, particularly those with a federal structure. However, it includes transfers from the central to the state and local governments; and the central government accounts for most of the changes in the budgetary stance. State-owned enterprises are generally also excluded from these figures, except those that perform governmental functions (such as food-manage-

ment agencies), but net payments or receipts between the central government and state-owned enterprises are included. See Floyd et al.1984.

11. Mexico's central government deficit continued to rise, largely because of external debt-service requirements in conjunction with the continuing depreciation of the Mexican peso, which insofar as it exceeded inflation raised the relative internal burden of the external debt service. In terms of the primary budget deficit—that is, the deficit excluding interest payments on internal and external public debt—Mexico shows a sharp decline in the deficit, more than 15 percentage points of GDP, rather than the rise shown in table 3.5. Brazil had a more modest decline. On the operational deficit—that is, the deficit excluding the inflation component of interest payments (which represent amortization of the debt in real terms), both countries show modest declines. See Cardoso and Dantas on Brazil and Beristain and Trigueros on Mexico in Williamson 1990.

12. More precisely, $g = 6.6 - .92(SEE)$, where g is the exponential growth rate of real GDP of each of our countries over the period 1980–88 and SEE is the standard deviation of the residuals of each of the time-series equations used to derive g. A standard error of 2 percentage points is thus associated with a reduction of the trend growth rate by 1.84 percentage points. For this cross-sectional equation, $R2 = 0.37$ and the t statistic for the coefficient on SEE is 3.1.

13. Growing low-income countries can be expected to have higher rates of inflation than high-income countries, without reflecting any loss of competitiveness, as a result of the impact of rising wages on the service component of the consumer price index or the GNP deflator.

Chapter 4

1. Unfortunately, the definition of "developing countries" is not uniform in all sources on the question of debt. The International Monetary Fund, for instance, includes a few Eastern European

countries and China in this category. The United Nations excludes these countries. For most purposes here, all indebted developing countries will be used to include the usual group of countries designated as developing countries less seven or eight major oil-producing countries in the Middle East. When the IMF is the source, the figures will also include data on a few Eastern European countries.

2. See IMF, *International Capital Markets: Developments and Prospects,* Washington, D.C., April 1990, table A28.

3. Two other widely used sources were also too optimistic. The December 1981 OECD forecast was for a decline of U.S. GNP in the first half of 1982, but for a sharp recovery in the second half, yielding a 0.5 percent decline for all of 1982 compared with 1981.

By April 1982, well into the recession, the IMF forecast a year-over-year decline of 1.0 percent. In the event, the actual decline was 2.5 percent. See OECD, *Economic Outlook,* December 1981, p. 12; and IMF, *World Economic Outlook,* April 1982, appendix table 1.

4. See, for example, Diaz-Alejandro 1983, Fishlow 1985, and Eichengreen in Edwards and Larrain 1989.

Chapter 5

1. See Lomax 1986 for a convenient summary of thirty-three proposals.

2. The *New Republic* (July 28, 1986, p. 9) expressed strong approval; economist William Cline (*Washington Post,* July 15, 1986) expressed strong disapproval.

3. A global framework such as Bradley's could of course be applied on a case-by-case basis, but in that event the "formula" approach is unduly limiting.

4. Enders and Mattione (1984, pp.47–50) give some illustrative calculations of the impact on GNP in seven Latin American coun-

tries over the period 1983–87 of a hypothetical debt repudiation at the end of 1982. Venezuela improves its position substantially, Argentina and Brazil improve their positions slightly, and the remaining four countries are made substantially worse off in terms of GNP growth. But note that the authors hypothesize debt repudiation, not conciliatory selective nonpayment.

Brazil in early 1987 announced that for an indefinite period it would suspend interest payments on bank debt. To avoid seizure of official reserves, it moved them to the Bank for International Settlements, thus foregoing substantial interest earnings.

Interest rates charged on trade credits and interbank debt, which continued to be serviced, rose significantly. Brazil thus lost over two billion dollars in interest paid or foregone and in loss of trade credit. President Sarney is reported to have said later that it was the worst decision he made.

5. See Rieffel 1986. For the largest debtors, the sequence has been reversed (IMF program first, followed by a meeting with commercial bank creditors, followed by a Paris Club meeting), because official credits are less important than commercial bank credits.

6. Fund credit outstanding was about $32 billion in December 1989, compared with usable resources of about $70 billion, not counting the various special borrowing arrangements that are available under certain conditions.

7. Ten in Latin America plus Ivory Coast, Morocco, Nigeria, the Philippines, and Yugoslavia.

8. Bank for International Settlements, *Annual Report*, June 1990, p.132.

9. This figure includes scheduled amortization payments that probably would not have occurred through "normal" rescheduling. The interest equivalent saving was about $1.5 billion a year.

10. In the form of permitted purchases of market-discounted debt in the case of the Philippines.

11. See Kenen 1990; also Twentieth Century Fund1989. A version of this proposal was made by Kenen in a column in The *New York Times* in March 1983. At that time he spoke of a discount of only 10 percent.

12. Using a regression equation by Sachs and Huizinga (1987) to estimate the price of commercial bank claims in the secondary market, William Cline has shown that the actual debt-to-GDP ratios remain well below the magnitude of 1.8 to 2.7 that would be required for Kenen's contention to hold. In other words, writing off some debt would reduce the total market value of outstanding debt. See Cline 1989.

13. Prices quoted in the secondary market for bank debt do not represent an accurate valuation of that debt. Some banks sell claims in that market to rid themselves of the nuisance and sometimes opprobrium of continuing to carry them. Other banks believe the claims to be more valuable. In a properly functioning market, the second (larger) group of banks should *buy* claims in the market, thus bidding up their value. But they are reluctant to do so given the adverse publicity that would probably engender and the regulatory requirement to add to their reserves.

14. It should be noted that much of the "capital flight" from developing countries was quite legal under the prevailing laws both of the sending and of the receiving countries. Argentina, Chile, Mexico, and Venezuela, in particular, permitted private export of capital around 1980. Under different circumstances, it would be praised as sensible diversification of portfolios. But it is likely that some of it was not legal, and most of it continues to avoid or evade domestic taxation. Some Latin American countries do not even in principle tax the earnings on overseas investments by residents; others, while formally creating a tax liability, have no mechanism for enforcement.

15. An interesting development that involves some effective writedown of debt, some repatriation of resident capital, and some conversion of debt for equity has been introduced in different

variants by Chile, Argentina, Mexico, and the Philippines. A stylized version of these debt-to-equity policies has the country's central bank stand willing to buy back debtor-country external debt at a discount in exchange for local currency that is used for approved equity investments. The official discount is, however, less than the market discount on such debt. A Mexican resident, for example, might buy a U.S. bank claim of $10 million on Mexico for $5 million, and then sell it to the Bank of Mexico for the equivalent of $7.5 million in Mexican pesos, valued at the going exchange rate. The transaction thus extinguishes the external dollar debt of $10 million with $5 million of resident funds held abroad. This type of transaction of course presupposes a U.S. bank willing to sell its claim at a discount—moral hazard is severe here, because that willingness is presumably influenced by Mexican policies—and a Mexican resident willing to return funds held abroad at an implicit exchange rate more attractive than the going market rate A serious disadvantage of debt-for-equity swaps is that they may be inflationary, insofar as the domestic currency counterpart of the foreign debt adds to the money supply; and it may add to the budget deficit, insofar as high-interest domestic debt is enlarged to reduce low-interest foreign debt. Both problems can be avoided if the government sells its state enterprises for foreign debt, as Argentina began to do in 1990.

16. A more complete list of possible actions to provide future financing for developing countries can be found in Bergsten, Cline, and Williamson 1985 and in Lessard and Williamson 1985.

17. The bonds of the African Development Bank, for instance, are rated AA+ despite a poor portfolio of doubtful project loans.

18. Total arrears reached $18 billion in early 1990, according to the Institute of International Finance.

References

Asher, Robert E., and Edward S. Mason. 1973. *The World Bank since Bretton Woods*. Washington, D.C.: Brookings Institution.

Bergsten, C.F., William Cline, and John Williamson. 1985. *Bank Lending to Developing Countries: The Policy Alternatives*. Washington, D.C.: Institute for International Economics.

Balassa, Bela. 1989. *New Directions in World Economy*. London: Macmillan.

Bossons, John, Rudiger Dornbusch, and Stanley Fischer, eds. 1986. *Essays in Macroeconomics and Finance*. Cambridge, MA: MIT Press.

Cline, William. 1984. *International Debt: Systemic Risk and Policy Response*. Washington, D.C.: Institute for International Economics.

Cline, William R. 1989. "The International Debt Problem: Status, Analytical Issues, and Policy," (May), processed. Washington, D. C.: Institute for International Economics.

Connolly, Michael. 1989. "Macroeconomic Policies, Adjustment, and Long-Run Growth in Cameroon." World Bank mss. Washington, D.C.

Cooper, Richard N. 1977. "A New International Economic Order for Mutual Gain." *Foreign Policy* (Spring).

Cooper, Richard N., and Jeffrey Sachs. 1985. "Borrowing Abroad: The Debtor's Perspective." In *International Debt and the Developing Countries*, ed. G. W. Smith and J. T. Cuddington. Washington, D.C.: World Bank.

Corbo, Vittorio, Jaime de Melo, and James Tybout. 1986. "What Went Wrong with the Recent Reforms in the Southern Cone?" *Economic Development and Cultural Change* 34 (April): 607–640.

Corden, W. M. 1990. "Macroeconomic Policy and Growth: Some Lessons from Experience." *World Bank Economic Review*. Washington, D.C.

Corden, W. M., and J. P. Neary. 1982. "Booming Sector and De-Industrialization in a Small Open Economy." *Economic Journal* 92 (December).

Diaz-Alejandro, Carlos. 1983. "Stories of the 1930s for the 1980s." In *Financial Policies and the World Capital Market: The Problem of Latin American Countries*, ed. Pedro Aspe Armella, et al. Chicago: University of Chicago Press.

Dornbusch, Rudiger. 1988. *Exchange Rates and Inflation*. Cambridge, MA: MIT Press.

Edwards, Sebastian, and Felipe Larrain, eds. 1989. *Debt, Adjustment, and Recovery*. Cambridge, MA: Basil Blackwell.

Eichengreen, Barry, and Richard Portes. 1986. "Debt and Default in the 1930s: Causes and Consequences." *European Economic Review* 30: 559-640.

Enders, Thomas O., and Richard P. Mattione. 1984. *Latin America, The Crisis of Debt and Growth*. Washington, D.C.: Brookings Institution.

Feinberg, Richard, and Valeriana Kallab, eds. 1984. *Adjustment Crisis in the Third World*. Washington, D. C.: Overseas Development Council.

Fishlow, Albert. 1985. "Lessons from the Past: Capital Markets during the Nineteenth Century and the Interwar Period." *International Organization* 39 (Summer): 383–440.

Floyd, Robert H., Clive S. Gray, and R. P. Short. 1984. *Public Enterprise in Mixed Economies.* Washington, D.C.: International Monetary Fund.

Foreign Bondholders Protective Council. *Annual Report for 1939.* New York.

Gil-Diaz, Francisco. 1987. "Some Lessons from Mexico's Tax Reform." In *The Theory of Taxation for Developing Countries,* ed. David Newbury and Nicholas Stern. Oxford: Oxford University Press.

Gardner, Richard N., S. Okita, and B. J. Udink. 1975. *The Trilateral World and the Developing Countries: New Arrangements for Cooperation, 1976–1980.* New York: Trilateral Commission.

Gastil, Raymond D. 1987. *Freedom in the World.* New York: Greenwood Press.

Gwin, Catherine, Richard E. Feinberg, and others. 1989. *The International Monetary Fund in a Multipolar World: PullingTogether.* Washington, D.C.: Overseas Development Council.

Hiey, Jacques Pegatienan. 1987. *Ivory Coast.* Helsinki: WIDER.

International Monetary Fund. *World Economic Outlook.* Washington, D.C., April 1990.

Kaletsky, Anatole. 1985. *The Costs of Default.* New York: Priority Press.

Kenen, Peter B. 1990. "Organizing Debt Relief: The Need for a New Institution." *Journal of Economic Perspectives* 4 (Winter): 7–18.

Krueger, Anne O. 1978. *Foreign Trade Regimes and Economic Development: Liberalization Attempts and Consequences.* Lexington, MA: Ballinger.

Lancaster, Carol, and John Williamson, eds. 1986. *African Debt and Financing*. Washington, D.C.: Institute for International Economics.

Lessard, Donald R., and John Williamson. 1985. *Financial Intermediation Beyond the Debt Crisis*. Washington, D.C.: Institute for International Economics.

Lessard, Donald, and John Williamson, eds. 1987. *Capital Flight and Third World Debt*. Washington, D.C.: Institute for International Economics.

Levy, Walter J. 1974. "World Oil Cooperation or International Chaos." *Foreign Affairs* (July): 690–713.

Little, I. M. D. 1982. *Economic Development: Theory, Policy, and International Relations*. New York: Basic Books.

Little, Ian, Tibor Scitovsky, and Maurice Scott. 1970. *Industrialization and Trade in Some Developing Countries*. New York: Oxford Unversity Press.

Lomax, David F. 1986. *The Developing Country Debt Crisis*. London: Macmillan.

Lynn, Robert, and F. Desmond McCarthy. 1989. "Recent Economic Performance of Developing Countries." Working Paper 228. Washington, D.C.: World Bank.

Michaely, Michael, Demetris Papageorgiou, and Aremeane M. Choksi. 1991. *Liberalizing Foreign Trade: Lessons of Experience in the Developing World*. Cambridge, MA: Basil Blackwell.

Phelps, Edmond S. 1978. "Commodity Supply Shocks and Full Employment Monetary Policy." *Journal of Money, Credit, and Banking* (May).

Rieffel, Alexis. 1986. "The Role of the Paris Club in Managing Debt Problems." *Princeton Essays in International Finance* 161.

Sachs, Jeffrey D. 1984. "Theoretical Issues in International Borrowing." *Princeton Studies in International Finance* 54.

Sachs, Jeffrey, and Harry Huizinga. 1987. "U.S. Commercial Banks and the Developing Country Debt Crisis." *Brookings Papers on Economic Activity* 2: 555–606.

Schultze, Charles, and Robert Z. Lawrence, eds. 1987. *Barriers to European Growth*. Washington, D.C.: Brookings Institution.

Twentieth Century Fund. 1989. *The Road to Economic Recovery*. New York.

United Nations. 1986, 1988. *World Economic Survey*.

United Nations Conference on Trade and Development (UNCTAD). 1986, 1989. *Trade and Development Report*.

Williamson, John, ed. 1983. *IMF Conditionality*. Washington, D.C.: Institute for International Economics.

Williamson, John, ed. 1990. *Latin American Adjustment*. Washington, D.C.: Institute for International Economics.

World Bank. 1990. *World Bank Development Report 1989*. New York: Oxford University Press.

World Bank. 1986. *Financing Adjustment with Growth in Sub-Saharan Africa*.

Index